~~Dear Dale~~,

Confidently yours—
Sheila Kennedy

1

FOREWORD BY BERT MARTINEZ

AMERICA'S MOST TRUSTED BUSINESS GENERATOR

CHOICES
TO CHANGES

THE Confidence Coach Shares the Practices Of Confident Entrepreneurs

Sheila Kennedy

Choices to Changes

THE Confidence Coach Shares the Practices of Confident Entrepreneurs

©2015 by Sheila Kennedy

Expert Insights Publishing
1001 East WT Harris Blvd. #247
Charlotte, NC 28213

ISBN: 13:978-1515171881

ISBN-10:1515171884

Author: Sheila Kennedy
Foreword: Bert Martinez
Cover Photography: Jenniffer Merida
Edited by: Joy Underhill

Dedication

Without these three men, this book would not be in your hands. I am so grateful.

To my Inner Circle. You inspire me every day. Your unwavering support sees me through. Can't imagine life without you. #ironsharpensiron

To my brother, Tom Kennedy. Without your observations and questions, this book definitely would not have become the project it did. You challenge me and spur me on to deliver a better product every time. I value your guidance and mentorship.

To James Malinchak, the founder of Big Money Speaker Boot Camp, featured on America's Secret Millionaire. Attending your boot camp changed the way I saw many things related to my business. The experience and exposure to you and the other leaders you had speak changed the way I think, feel, and practice. This project has been such a blessing because of the experience you created at boot camp. Thank you.

Acknowledgements

Shannon, my daughter, who has endured the ups and downs of this past year. You are my inspiration. I do what I do so you can have a better life. I love you more Nani Kai!

My family – You provide more than I have the right to ask. I am so grateful for your love and support.

The TWELVE Confident Entrepreneurs – Thank you from the bottom of my heart for saying "YES!" and demonstrating so flawlessly how confident entrepreneurship works! It is such an honor to share your stories with the world. I am humbled and inspired by each of you!

Kim Boudreau Smith, Abby Kohut and Christine Baker Marriage – Thank you for sharing your zebra moments with me! You all are beautiful examples of what happens when you lead with your why!

Joy Underhill of Words by Joy – You are a rock star editor. Thank you for meeting crazy deadlines and having the right words to fill in the gap. I am so very grateful.

Jenniffer Merida of PhotoChica. You make me look good – here is to having an amazing photographer.

Robin Taney of Studio4PR. You are the GET REAL Girl! Thank you for being firm and helping me see what I couldn't or didn't want to. Can't imagine how I would have accomplished this without your guidance and expertise in publicity.

Bible Study Beauties – Some of my favorite moments over the last year were spent with you. Thank you for your love, support and prayers!

Steve Catan, My godfather, for whispering in my ear, "Go do the Big Thing!"

B.V. and the conversation that started it all! Thank you for sharing your needs with me! Look at what came of it!

All my clients, past and present – What I observe in you helped create the foundation of the content for this book. I am so grateful that you have been open to sharing and getting messy with me. I am honored by your trust and grateful for your hunger to do more and achieve more. You inspire me!

Foreword

By Bert Martinez

Imagine this scenario. What if everyone you met was attracted to you? What if you were a sought-after thought leader in your industry? What if fear and rejection could not hold you back?

Sounds a bit too far-fetched to be true? I thought so too until I discovered confidence!

Confidence is that magical mystical element that can turn a nobody into a somebody. Otherwise, how would you explain Arnold Schwarzenegger's unstoppable multi successful careers?

Confident entrepreneurs are the go-getters that make the impossible possible. Steve Jobs, Oprah Winfrey, and Elon Musk are just a few examples of what can be achieved when one has confidence in themselves, in their systems, and in their dreams!

When you are confident the universe opens up to you and everything seems to work in your favor.

The Law of Attraction works faster when you have belief and belief grows out of confidence. In this book you will discover 12 amazing stories of entrepreneurs that will inspire you to cultivate your confidence and to change your life.

The content of this book is worth millions of dollars! This book has the potential making your life and your business richer than you could ever imagine.

I would recommend you, the reader, go through this book a minimum of three times and master the strategies contained therein.

Again I ask you imagine a life where fear didn't stop you, where people were instantly attracted to you, that you were the sought after thought leader of your industry, and a celebrity in your niche.

That is what awaits you in the pages of this book!

Table of Contents

Introduction

I am the lead-by-example girl.

When I started my first career 20 years ago as a life skills instructor for the U.S. Army, I worked for a program that taught and mentored young soldiers, their spouses, and DA civilians in the skills necessary to be self-sufficient leaders, problem solvers, and communicators.

It was important to the senior leaders to pass on the information they learned through their experiences, and the participant's results were outstanding. That example stuck with me and I have crafted my coaching practice to share what I have learned in hopes that it shortens the learning curve and reduces some of the pain and fear of those who follow.

I have not always been the confident entrepreneur I am today. In 2008 when I started my home staging and redesign company, it appeared I had the perfect life. I seemed to be happily married, had a big house, financial security, and was well respected in the community.

Behind closed doors, life wasn't so perfect. No marriage is, but ours had some significant problems that I carefully concealed. I was a business owner living in the entrepreneurial fishbowl, and if I shared how messed up my personal life had become, people might not do business with me. I couldn't risk that, so I put a smile on my face and carried on.

I eventually left what had turned into an abusive situation. My self-esteem was at an all-time low. I did what I had to do to survive each day but there was not much energy or creativity left over to build my business and be a mother to my daughter. I took a job selling furniture so that we could eat. I kept my business open hoping that something would happen that would catapult me to success. I studied the how-to of building a business but something was still missing.

I realized I would never create a better business if I didn't build confidence in myself. I knew strategies to build the business, but I lacked the confidence to support and sustain them. Desperate to make a better life, I began my quest to discover how to build the self-confidence I had so little of.

It was hard work to build that kind of confidence and required all of the tenacity and resilience I could muster. That quest turned into a new coaching practice and ultimately my book, *You Had It All Along, 5 Keys to Unlocking the POWER of Confidence at your Core*. I wrote the book as a blueprint for others to build their confidence so they could live the life they desired.

About a year after the book came out, I had hosted an event teaching how to gain visibility and have the confidence to sustain it for my local community. One of the participants had read *You Had It All Along* and mentioned that it was great, but was work she had done years prior. She voiced that she needed a book about how to be a confident entrepreneur. Little did I know how that conversation would spark a new quest to clearly define exactly what being a confident entrepreneur means.

I started writing this book a year ago. I thought I knew everything I wanted to share. Between my own practice and attitudes and the observations I made in my clients, I thought I had a pretty good handle on what confident entrepreneurship was all about. This past year has been enlightening to say the least. I learned every lesson that I write about in a very intimate way.

The book you are holding in your hand is a testimony that confident entrepreneurship actually works. After interviewing the twelve entrepreneurs for the book, I needed to raise the funds to have it published. Instead of taking out a loan or crowdsourcing, I conducted a 60-day experiment employing the practices that had been shared.

The results were outstanding! I tripled my income from the 60 days prior to that. I attracted my ideal clients. I accepted speaking engagements and things were going well at home.

When the sixty days were over, I'm not sure if I got cocky, busy or lazy, but I let some of the practices slide. I didn't keep up and neither did my success. This book almost didn't happen because of a lack of resources and, at times, a lack of confidence. Unwilling to let the project go, I once again adopted the practices in this book, regained my footing, and love the results. I am confident that the practices outlined here work; you are holding the proof in your hands.

The Entrepreneurs

Early on in the book's formation, someone shared with me that I couldn't write this book. I wasn't really a confident entrepreneur, because if I was, I would be more financially successful. My lack of financial success would send the signal that I wasn't a credible confident entrepreneur, so entrepreneurs would not read the book.

Determined to share the lessons I have learned about confident entrepreneurship, I thought about how I could tell the story so that more entrepreneurs would want to read it. I understood that some people would equate financial success with confidence (even though they're very different things), so I made a list of traits that a confident entrepreneur possesses. Then I asked entrepreneurs who possess those traits and have also achieved financial success to share their practices as well.

The Twelve Entrepreneurs spotlighted in this book have had varying degrees of financial success and confidence levels throughout their careers. After conducting all of the interviews, I found that most had in common the same practices as I had planned to share. Our common practices can be found in the body of the book. Each entrepreneur had practices or stories that were unique to them and that is what is found in their individual spotlights.

I asked twelve questions during the interviews. You may find them interesting and an opportunity for a little self-discovery. They could certainly be used as a tool to identify your own practice of confident entrepreneurship.

1. How did you enter entrepreneurship?
2. Have you always felt confident?

3. Has entrepreneurship always gone as planned? Has there ever been a time when you questioned what you were doing?
4. While you are building your business, what keeps you focused and inspired?
5. What is your *why*?
6. Are there certain practices you employ to keep your business growing?
7. Who are your mentors?
8. What is your practice of self-care and does it impact your business?
9. Change and growth can be difficult for people. How do you handle change and growth and how do you assist your customers or clients to do the same?
10. Of the five keys to unlocking the POWER of confidence at your core, which key has impacted you and your business the most?
11. How do you respond to naysayers and haters?
12. If you could pass on one lesson to the reader, what would it be?

I believe that the measure of success for these entrepreneurs is worth noting. Similar to my own, the measure of success for the confident entrepreneurs in this book was not merely financial. It involved asking:

•   Did I influence a life?

•   Did I do something that I was afraid to do before?

•   Did I reach out and share this product, service or offering and be of service in a bigger way?

•   Did I take a step closer to living my purpose?

Money was not the primary reason for doing what they do. Of course they are all business owners and making money is a part of what they do, but their success was closely related to their *why*. It had more to do with influence and impact than it did money.

Choices to Changes

As their impact and influence grow and they become more trusted in the marketplace, they are given more financial responsibility to steward. The whole package – impact, fulfillment and profitability- has arrived, not because they are lucky, but because they exemplify the practices of confident entrepreneurs.

Part I: The Confident Entrepreneur

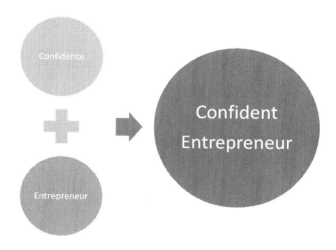

Each person has a back story that shapes who they are. The Confident Entrepreneur is no different. This section provides the background about what confidence is, who an entrepreneur is, what happens when you put the two of them together and why it matters. Find out what choices they make and what changes those choices turn into.

Lastly you will examine the POWER process which is the foundation of every entrepreneur's confidence.

Choices to Changes

Why Confident Entrepreneurship Matters

"If you want to make the world a better place, unleash an army of entrepreneurs. They are people who go out and fix things. They solve problems and get it done. We need to enable and help as many of them as we can." ~
Jeff Hoffman, Co-founder of Priceline.com and Color Jar.

The greatest help to an entrepreneur is to teach them how to practice confidently. So many entrepreneurs have how-to and logistical knowledge but lack the confidence to execute and sustain what they have learned. It's difficult to build a business without the right tools, and confidence is the most important tool available to you.

Confident Entrepreneurship is the organization of mindset, connections, and structure that provides the platform you need to change the world, no matter how big the world is you're trying to change. Success, however you define it, can be yours as you adopt these practices. In this book, you'll see examples of twelve entrepreneurs who have done just that.

If you want to share something with the world, whether it's a new toilet paper brand or a cure for cancer, recognize that it's a gift that has been given to you. The practices of confident entrepreneurs outlined here will help you organize and build the platform you need to share your gift.

Having the desire to inspire change does not mean you automatically do it in a way that makes it meaningful to anyone else. Changing people is a huge responsibility and comes with its own set of guidelines and accountability. The practices in this book will define these guidelines and give you the support that you can use when you're uncertain of your next move.

Think of **Confident Entrepreneurship** as the foundation on which you will stand to become courageous, intolerant, and strong enough to take the leap and fly.

The pieces of the foundation are important – even the seemingly insignificant ones. The methods of delivery and structure can be individualized to you, but the foundational practices will be the same. When these pieces are organized and aligned, you'll hit your sweet spot to enjoy the freedom and success that entrepreneurship brings.

Changing how people think, feel and behave requires a certain level of organization. In this book, you'll learn how to organize your thoughts, environment, systems, and relationships so you're free to take the risks that successful entrepreneurship dictates. You don't have to know how the organization will ultimately look, but it will likely get messy before it gets orderly. It's about subtracting what doesn't serve you and filling the empty space with the things that support your platform and contribute to forward movement.

There's a difference in the way entrepreneurs practice. Confident entrepreneurs are not defined by fear and insecurity and know they will be supported when they take risks. Confused entrepreneurs are led by indecision, fear, and uncertainty about their next steps. If you want to share your message but don't know how to set up the structure or build the relationships to achieve success on your terms, read on.

Confident Entrepreneurship involves taking risks and making choices to propel businesses forward. To build meaningful relationships, grow financially, and have more influence, practice like a confident entrepreneur!

Choices to Changes

Building confidence isn't as elusive as it may seem. In fact, the fastest way to create it is this:

Frame everything as a choice.

This may sound like an annoying practice, but it creates great impact. *Choosing* is an empowering activity. Embrace it!

Choices are the cornerstone of confidence. The way you choose – or struggle to make choices - forms the foundation for what will flow. If you can't find a way to make choices, your entrepreneurial desires will come to a standstill.

Choosing is a practice - and one of the most important practices you can adopt. When you're challenged in making choices, the whole entrepreneurial process gets backed up. Your attitude about your decision-making directly impacts the changes you're capable of making for yourself and those you are trying to reach. If you want to be successful in entrepreneurship, you must learn how to facilitate change for people even if all you want them to do is change their minds about a particular brand they use.

As an entrepreneur, the choices you make impact not just you and your business or enterprise. The marketplace and the global economy are impacted as well. You may want to serve a small population, but it still will have global impact.

When seen through a global lens, your choices are much more important even when that wasn't your intention. By adopting the practices of those who have achieved success, you can build a foundation of trust in yourself and know that your community and your source will support you – whether you define it as God, the universe, natural law, the spirit world or any other definition of a higher power.

Choices to Changes describes the process of becoming a confident entrepreneur. This involves summoning the power to choose and trusting that the resulting changes will be possible and supported. Confident entrepreneurs believe and trust that they will survive their own changes and facilitate change in others.

Confidence is not a destination or an absolute. If it were, then no changes would have to be made. Confidence is choosing to open the tool chest of skills and strategies you have acquired to ease the discomfort of growth. Confident entrepreneurs trust that they will possess what they need to make sound decisions and navigate the changes that take place as a result.

More and more people are trying entrepreneurism as a profession. Some will succeed and others will fail. Those who fail will do so not because they aren't capable. They will fail because they don't embrace the core of entrepreneurial success: the confidence to make choices and create lasting change.

Spotlight: Viki Winterton

*Viki Winterton easily demonstrates the spirit of what **Choices to Changes** is all about. She makes choices every day that impact the changes the people around her make.*

Viki Winterton, the founder of Expert Insights Publishing, believes that she is genetically wired for entrepreneurship. Her father was an entrepreneur and Viki attributes her love of freedom and adventure to her exposure of his entrepreneurial spirit as a child. The freedom that entrepreneurship provides has become her passion and motivator throughout her career.

Starting out as a young model, Viki occasionally worked odd part time jobs to support herself. One of those jobs was at an Ad Agency. She eventually soaked up enough experience and knowledge to go off on her own at 24 years old and start her own ad agency. Within two years, Viki's agency experienced such explosive growth that she sold it. Achieving eight figures in less than three years by someone who had no formal training in Advertising or had never owned a business before is quiet the achievement.

Growth is something that most desire, but Viki shared that she would have been more strategic about how fast that first company grew if she could do it again. It grew so fast it was out of integrity with Viki's initial vision and that was difficult for her, leading to her decision to let it go. Acting in the highest integrity is of utmost importance to her and something she has absolute confidence that she delivers daily.

Passion is what drives Viki and has delivered success despite a lack formal training at times. So often entrepreneurs fear stepping up because they do not have enough expertise, but Viki believes:

You can always learn what you need to know, but you can't learn passion.

When passion drives you, you give 150%. When you do that, you can always walk away from something that doesn't work out the way you planned, knowing you gave it your all. When giving less than 100%, there is room for doubt if things don't work out.

Following her passion and giving it her all have left no room for self-doubt.

Viki certainly makes the case for the balance of masculine and feminine energy. As she grows in wisdom, Viki no longer feels the need to push for clarity. When she is unclear or lacks direction in a project, she walks away from it and takes a couple days off. She opens herself up to creativity and intuition and proceeds from there.

Allowing flexibility with her vision usually results in the original vision being a small part of the whole successful project. If she remained rigid with her vision, she would not create the space for better things than she ever imagined.

Viki shares a quote "**Follow your bliss**" by one of her favorite mentors, Joseph Campbell. Connecting people with mentors that share ideas, resources and solutions to the challenges and questions people have is a strong desire for Viki. Always having been a strong advocate of having mentors and being a mentor, Viki loves seeing her vision come to life with Expert Insights Publishing. Following her bliss is not only a guiding principle for Viki, but also her measure of success. It is clear that the explosive growth she experienced in her ad agency, the consulting she did for decades and now Expert Insights Publishing makes the case for following your passion to achieve amazing results.

The Question of Confidence

There are many misconceptions about confidence. To understand how important your choices are, let's take confidence to its base level.

Confidence is *not* the same as self-esteem.

The word confidence comes from the Latin base word *confidere*, which means *to trust*. Taking confidence back to its root, **confidence is trusting that you are supported** and have everything you need in each moment of your life. Self-esteem, on the other hand, is believing that you are worthy of support.

That changes things quite a bit. If confidence is about trust, then it follows that there are going to be some areas of your life and enterprise where you will be more confident than others. In other words, you will always have areas of high confidence, like driving or reading.

You can never negatively judge yourself for not having confidence because there are areas of your life that you do. It is easy to dismiss those areas because there's nothing bringing them top of mind ... until something happens to shake your confidence and bring on fear and doubt.

You most likely drive every day without thinking twice about it. You've long since forgotten the fear and thrill when you first learned how to drive. You've forgotten that you first drove in an empty parking lot because that felt much safer than driving on the road. You dismiss that you drove back roads for quite a while until you got used to maneuvering a car in traffic.

Today, it is second nature to drive and you would deem yourself a confident driver. You have already passed from fear into confidence and are enjoying the freedom that driving affords you.

Yes, driving is easy - until you lose your headlights in a snowstorm. Then fear and insecurity roar loudly in your head. You still have choices. You can sit on the side of the road and wait it out. You can also open the tool chest of skills you've accumulated and cautiously proceed because you believe that arriving at your destination is more important than sitting on the side of the road waiting until it's safer.

Entrepreneurship is no different. You have a destination in mind. You can sit on the sidelines hoping that conditions will be right to move forward, or you can draw from what you already possess and choose to take action. It may not be an easy path and it certainly won't look like you expect it to, but with perseverance and trust, you will eventually arrive.

Imagine that confidence is the paint you apply to a canvas on which you are going to create a masterpiece. You might be tempted to paint confidence with a broad stroke that covers the entire canvas, but it doesn't really work that way. That broad stroke leaves you with a colored canvas that lacks depth or vibrancy because there are no highlights or shadows.

Picture confidence as the colors, highlights, and shadows you will paint your canvas with. Some colors will be easy to apply and others will require work for a very long time to get it just right.

Like paint, confidence is fluid. One tiny mistake with the brush can alter the whole work. It is self-esteem that reminds you that no matter what confidence has been created, your canvas always has been and still is quite beautiful.

The logo for my coaching practice illustrates this well. When I first started my coaching practice, I explained to the designer that I wanted just a logotype and no graphics. I was very surprised when this is what came back.

I loved the design but was curious as to why he created this instead of what I wanted. He picked a messy paint splatter because artists can make a brilliant and unexpected painting out of a drip or a mis-stroke of the brush. He said that is what I was trying to convey: to make a masterpiece out of your mess.

I have learned that **we are going to make messes, but we can turn them into masterpieces if we trust that we have the ability to do so**. For most, it's in your best interest to invite some of the messiness in, just so you can marvel at how it all turns out.

In entrepreneurism, there are going to be areas where you're extremely confident and can act automatically. These come second nature to you and you enjoy them.

In areas where you feel less confident, you can follow the practices of confident entrepreneurs to formulate new strategies and continually fill the tool chest with new skills to be better prepared for what comes next. You trust that even if you don't have everything you need at a given moment, you can gain access to it and will be supported in your every need. The result may not look like you want it to and you may not even like it, but that does not negate the fact that you will be supported. The resources you need will show up. It is your job to remain open to the possibilities because resources do not always look the way you expect them to.

Some believe that confidence is a shield that protects you from ever feeling fear and doubt. Nothing could be further from the truth.

Fear and insecurity exist because you feel unsafe. They are your body's way of keeping you safe and within your comfort zone. Any time you try something new or stretch out of your comfort zone, fear and doubt will show up. The measure of your confidence is not the absence or presence of fear and doubt, but rather how long you let them stay.

Each of the entrepreneurs in this book has met fear and doubt at some point in their careers. What's different about them is that they allowed fear and doubt to visit only momentarily. That's right. They identified the fear, decided that they would not be defined by it, and moved through it. They embraced success and failure because they trusted that they would be supported in both.

It's awesome when support comes in a neat little package, but sometimes it shows up as lack and darkness and a lesson you get to learn. Think of each moment as a gift. You get to unwrap it and derive the lesson of the gift inside.

Sometimes you can see the gift only when you recognize the absence of it. You have no reason to believe that the support you have received in every moment of your life until now will end. Proceed confidently from here knowing that your need will be provided.

Spotlight: Jeff Hoffman

Jeff Hoffman exemplifies the true definition of confidence. He trusts that each encounter will work out for his benefit in some way. What is interesting about Jeff is that he didn't even realize how true to form to the base of confidence he operates. He learned that definition of confidence during his interview. He has always operated from a place of trust that he will be supported in each endeavor.

Driven by a strong desire to control his destiny, Jeff Hoffman left his corporate job and lives the essence of a serial entrepreneur. To create repeat businesses, he needed the comfort in risk-taking that only confidence delivers. Jeff trusts that if he surrounds himself with smart people and creates strong teams that work well together, he can accomplish his goals.

Jeff's attitude about failure is that it allows him to discover a new way not to do something. Now that he knows which way not to go, he still has plenty of new routes to try. Thomas Edison said, "I have not failed, I just found what won't work." That attitude has allowed Jeff to get comfortable with the risks that he takes and it certainly has paid off in his positions as co-founder of Priceline.com and   Color Jar.

Like many do, Jeff questioned his legacy. He has been financially blessed, but he wanted to leave a positive impact on the world other than making money.
He embarked on a three-year tour around the world, mentoring entrepreneurs, women, and youth. He wanted to give back by mentoring and also discover how else he could help them. Mentorship was a missing element for much of Jeff's career, which is why he feels so strongly about providing it for those who need it.

Jeff speaks about the practice of info-sponging that led to the founding of Priceline. Info-sponging is observing what is happening outside your industry and in the world, literally taking notes and then connecting the dots of random ideas to create new solutions. This is about noticing the changes that are happening in the world, getting excited about them, and making them fit in new ways. Hunting for changes rather than fearing them is Jeff's attitude and he surrounds himself with people who feel the same.

Customer intimacy is another practice Jeff employs. Get out of your office. Get off the phone. Get off the computer and go hang out with your customers. Get to know their needs and challenges so you know how to serve them best. This practice has been adopted by other entrepreneurs and is how Zappos and Walmart came into existence.

Jeff challenges entrepreneurs to find their golden purpose in life. Don't stop seeking until you find it. He attributes his success to loving what he does. When you're passionate about what you do and why you're doing it, you'll be willing to work hard and achieve great results.

Entrepreneur: A Definition

You've learned a bit about confidence, but before you move any further, let's define the term, *entrepreneur*.

The word itself is a relatively modern term. It's a combination of the French word *entreprendre* (to undertake) and the English word *enterprise*. Miriam Webster defines entrepreneur as one who **organizes, manages and assumes risks of a business or enterprise**.

Brett Nelson wrote in *Forbes.com* that entrepreneurs, in the purest sense, are those who identify a need and fill it. It is a primordial urge, independent of product, service, industry or market.

Howard Stevenson of Harvard Business School penned my favorite definition. He writes, "... Entrepreneurs see an opportunity and don't feel constrained from pursuing it because they lack resources."

Think about this. Entrepreneurs do not feel constrained because they **trust** that resources will appear when they need them. Entrepreneurs do not have to know how those resources will appear; they just have to answer the call.

For some, not answering the call to entrepreneurship is almost like a form of medieval torture. The desire to serve is innate for most entrepreneurs but the other skills necessary to be successful may not come as easily.

As you explore the practices of confident entrepreneurs in Part II, you may find that you're already using many of them. You may also find that some are foreign to you and may take time adopting.

Choices to Changes

Remember, change happens only when you create an environment for success. Please do not overhaul all of your systems and strategies tomorrow. Slow and steady yields the best results. You want these practices to become second nature and beneficial to your cause. Having them become another source of frustration or negative self-judgment defeats the purpose.

Repeat out loud:

- I will open my mind to the possibilities.

- I will say *yes* to that which will serve me and my audience best.

- I will risk learning new things to accomplish more than I imagined possible.

- I will not allow myself to choose defeat when success is very much an option.

Spotlight: David Dey

David Dey embodies the essence of a confident entrepreneur. He not only practices as an entrepreneur, but his mission is to assist other entrepreneurs to confidently practice so that they can create social change in their local and global communities.

David is founder of the Institute for Social Entrepreneurship, and from the time he was a kid, he knew he wanted to change the world and saw business as an opportunity to do just that.

Throughout his entrepreneurial career, David has been the consummate risk-taker. He continually puts the motto "**Without great risk, there is no great reward**" into practice. He doesn't fear that it may take more time than others are willing to wait. He understands how important the impact is that social entrepreneurship is making and he patiently accepts the risks of strategically promoting these ideas.

When it comes to risk-taking and connections, David sees the goal not as a destination, but as a refining process. He adds partners who will complement his skill set as he promotes the idea that entrepreneurship can be more than an endeavor to make money. Entrepreneurs can also use innovation and business skills to contribute to their community and solve complex community problems. Adaptive in methodology, David incorporates technology and various delivery methods to spread the reach of social entrepreneurship.

When David travels to a new community, he rents a car to explore and observe it, rather than going sightseeing. He watches for trends, facial expressions, interactions, and needs of those in the community. Then he seeks to serve and confidently connect the resources and businesses that can serve the community best - a critical aspect of his success.

David often connects with the "forgotten people" or those who are underserved to determine business models that will serve both the needs of such people and the entrepreneurs who will deliver products and services to the community.

David recognizes that sometimes the innovation he is introducing is too big of a stretch for the community. When that happens, he scales back the innovation to fit the understanding and comfort level of the community. He engages in the classic model of meeting people where they are, works with them to build their level of understanding, and supports them through the changes they make.

One of the remarkable things about David is that he doesn't stop doing what he believes in. He's been on this path for more than twenty years and it hasn't been an easy road. Only recently has social entrepreneurship been gaining recognition and incorporation on a global scale. He is highly adaptive, and when something he's doing isn't working, he finds a different way by refining and struggling to find the best results.

David does not shy away from what is difficult because he knows the payoff will be great. Honing his communication and active listening skills help him determine the next direction to take.

David doesn't sit around waiting for new opportunities. He gets going! "Seize the opportunities when you have them," he says. "The longer you wait, the harder it will be. Anything that involves changing people takes time. Don't waste your time or wish it away. It will take longer than you anticipate to accomplish change."

What Stands in Your Way

Choices are the cornerstone upon which we build the foundation of our confidence. We get to choose what we believe, what we fear, if we fear, how we behave, what we say, and the list goes on. Every action and reaction we have is a choice. You can't always choose yourself out of a situation, but you can choose your reaction. That's a powerful position to be in and changes the game completely.

Getting to choose is the basis for everything else, but what happens when we get stuck in decision-making? It can mean the slow death of entrepreneurs regardless of the value or quality of what they have to offer.

There are huge costs associated with not making decisions confidently. Consider just a few:

1.   **Missed opportunities**. It's hard to even quantify this. What could happen when you don't follow up with a new contact because you chose not to have an infrastructure that supports such activity? What happens when you choose not to go to a networking event that might be filled with your ideal client?

2.   **Missed deadlines**. This can impact your reputation and reliability. You can incur fees for paying bills late, plus it can lead to more missed opportunities.

3.   **The wrong environment**. If you're afraid to spend money or resources to update your environment – one that is lacking the tools and support you need to reach more people - what does that cost you in the end?

4.   **Paralysis by analysis**. Being informed and conducting research are great, but what happens when you get stuck in data

collection and can't actually move on to making decisions? Lost opportunities, dried-up resources, bored and unchallenged team members, frustration, and more. Are you beginning to see a pattern here?

Poor decision-making is not the only thing standing in your way. Consider these additional stumbling blocks.

Money.   Your best strategy is to heal any negativity you have with money and resources for doing so abound. Overcome the obstacles. Heal the wounds. Expose the doubts and fears. You can't reach the level of financial success you want until you develop a positive money mindset.

Time.   There are tons of resources on time management and it all boils down to this. You have the same 24 hours as everyone else. How you choose to spend that time is up to you. If you're not confident in deciding how best to invest your time, then you're going to have a hard time. It is more about managing your priorities than it is your time.

Cockiness. Confidence and cockiness are often confused. Cockiness is a veiled attempt to hide insecurity, hurt, and vulnerability.

Confidence is silent and insecurity is loud. That adage is so true. You don't talk about being a confident driver because you are one. When you are confident, you don't have a need to declare it.

Spend your time observing others and serving their needs rather than proving your value. Pay attention the next time you're at a networking event. Those who go on and on talking about their wonderful qualities are usually the ones who need convincing.

Spotlight: Karen McMillan

Karen McMillan understands what holds the entrepreneur back. She is a divine example of removing the obstacles, both real and perceived, to achieve a greater level of satisfaction and fulfillment in her practice.

Karen McMillan is a peaceful entrepreneur, due in large part to how she structures her environment. Both her internal and external environments contribute to her peaceful and mindful coaching practice.

Karen holds two titles: "Retreat Muse" and "YINpreneur™." She has the most unique set of skills. Building a platform for the practice of retreat – both virtual and land-based - is a part of it, but as the YINpreneur™, she is one of the most knowledgeable systems resources around.

Karen understands that building systems to support your business is the best invitation to the freedom entrepreneurship can provide. By using available technology, systematizing and streamlining her daily processes, she frees up time to pursue creativity, spend time with family, and engage in other activities. That single practice provides the opportunity to fill the unoccupied space with what she needs and desires – inner peace at her core. The push to be busy is gone because her systems create greater efficiency and productivity.

Karen believes in quiet time and exemplifies the practice of slowing down to speed up your success. Even as little as a five-minute mini-retreat can recharge the body and mind to enhance creativity and productivity. Cultivating an environment that nurtures and inspires retreat is one of the practices that she swears by because the results have been so powerful and long lasting.

Continuity in connections and building relationships with Self and others, are also important practices for Karen. Her authentic and heart-centered communication style is highly effective and seeds growth. Karen avoids sound bite and marketing copy, and in her authenticity, creates a loyal community. Real and open communication may not appeal to everyone, but it eliminates a "buy once and not again" mentality and fosters the gateway to a strong community.

Karen hesitated before throwing out her shingle as the YINpreneur™ and the Retreat Muse. Many people would not understand and could be vocal about their opposition. At one point Karen chose to listen to the naysayers and pulled back, thus mirroring her lack of confidence in the platform and services she was providing.

Still not feeling fulfilled, Karen chose to listen to her inner voice, and those who had been transformed by what she offers rather than those who didn't understand. Those transformations were the true measure of her potential.

Karen feels it's important to remember that confidence doesn't mean perfection. There's no need to take things so seriously because perfection is beyond our control. When you lack confidence, give in to the power of vulnerability. Allow for quiet and reject the busy-ness entrepreneurs often hide behind to find your path to peacefulness, productivity, and profitability. In addition, as Karen always reminds us, *remember to breathe*!

Standing in the Gap

Entrepreneurs believe they can do what hasn't been done before. To varying degrees, they believe they possess what they need to accomplish the tasks set before them.

By contrast, *confident* entrepreneurs trust that what they do not possess will find its way to them so they can fill the gap. This is an act of faith, regardless of how you define the word.

So what is the gap?

Think of the Grand Canyon. On one side, you know what you can accomplish due to your mindset or skill set. You acknowledge your strengths or weaknesses and realize how far they will get you. On the other side is your goal. More often than not, a gap exists between what you can do and what you want to achieve.

One thing's for sure: you won't be able to achieve your goals without assistance. You can't get there on your own.

So you can **stand in the gap and make a choice**. With most entrepreneurial decisions, you can:

- Decide to ask for help.

- Surrender control and see what comes to you.

- Get discouraged and change your goal.

- Become paralyzed with no movement either way because that's all you can do.

- Trust that what you need will arrive exactly when you need it, even if it doesn't look like you imagined it would.

Standing in the gap is where you get to fully engage your confidence. You know what you're capable of and you know what

47

your goal is, but there's a big gap between the two. You can close the gap by trusting that whatever you need would find its way to you.

Sometimes support is magical and just shows up unannounced – like getting new clients when it wasn't expected – but other times it is a little more discreet. Remember that you get to choose what you can do to make the impossible possible. You're not free to slack off because support will show up. The help is often contingent upon how much effort you put in.

Try asking yourself: **What or who are you trusting?** You may be uncomfortable with that question, but as a confident entrepreneur, you'll learn to get comfortable with the uncomfortable.

Maybe you trust in God. Perhaps you name it "Source," "Creator," "the Secret," "the Universe," "Natural Law," or a whole host of other things. Regardless of the name, it is how you explain why unexplainable things happen.

Call it what you will. The faith and trust that make up your confidence goes beyond yourself. If you haven't done so yet, this is a great time to begin exploring what you believe about explaining the unexplainable.

Let me draw from my own experience here. In 2012, I was a youth coach and hosted a Summer Lovin' Luau – a dance party for teenagers to teach them about chastity and modesty before they were released from school for the summer.

I came up with the idea, but didn't have any money and couldn't imagine how I would pull something like this off. I was at a stoplight one morning and the next thing I knew I was pulling into the parking lot of a National Guard Armory. I asked about renting the facility. The sergeant was totally on board, gave me use of the facility for free, and we chose a date just five weeks away.

I had no idea how I was going to make this happen. I said yes to the call, but I had no funds, no committees or staff and five weeks to plan. I was truly standing in the gap.

So I took to the streets of my small town wearing a lei and asking businesses and churches if they would support the event. I received $900 in monetary donations plus the food, drinks, goodie bags, and decorations. I received donations of media attention and clothes for a fashion show from The Gap that would feature modern clothing that was both modest and stylish. I charged $10 at the door and ended up donating $450 to a local Advocacy and Support Center that works with abused children.

It was an awesome night that defied a logical explanation. Yes, I had to hustle and do my part, but I believe God provided the rest of the resources until my every need was filled. It may appear that a teen dance party in rural Kentucky might not be making a huge global impact, but I beg to differ. I will never know the extent of the impact the event had on those who attended that night, but I do know the impact it had on me.

That night confirmed what I have been saying all along: **you will be supported in your need**. I didn't know how to make it happen. I just said yes to an idea and asked for help. Resources showed up one after another until my goal was achieved. The impossible became possible.

Success, as they say, begets success. I've gone on to create a coaching practice, have written two books, and I'm just getting started. It all began with trust as I stood in the gap.

Spotlight: Forbes Riley

Forbes Riley knows what it's like to stand in the gap. One of her guiding mantras is "leap and the net will appear." She lives that mantra every day and completely fits definition of confidence?

As successful, talented, and beautiful as Forbes is, even she has experienced challenges. The way she meets those challenges is as enterprising as her spirit. When she was mugged as a young woman, she took up martial arts, which she continues to practice today. When her family didn't have money to send her to college, she won a beauty pageant and financed her education herself. When her acting career didn't work out the way she had hoped, she branded herself as the "Pitch Queen" who has sold more than $2 billion dollars of products, leading to her current incredible success.

Forbes spent much of her career pitching fitness products on FIT TV and Home Shopping Network. She knew how to spot revolutionary products, and when she discovered the Spin Gym®, she used her informed and qualified opinion to declare that it would be the next best thing on the market. She even pitched the idea on Reality TV only to have it shot down. Forbes decided to finance the project herself, using everything she had because she believed in it that much.

Forbes believes that no isn't a negative, touting that it stands for Never-ending Opportunity. That mindset led her to stand in the gap when she tried to get financing and market the Spin Gym®. She had been told no by the Home Shopping Network, but that didn't deter her. She found another shopping network and asked for two minutes to sell twenty-five units – which she did. The next day, she sent out a press release announcing that the Spin Gym® sold out in its international launch on its first day. The rest is amazing history.

Forbes is a well-known actress and TV personality, and she reigns as the Pitch Queen. Her ease and flair for making a pitch started when she was a young girl. Her father was a frustrated inventor with several inventions that never happened because he didn't know how to promote them. He asked a young Forbes how to promote but she couldn't help him at the time. He died before any of his inventions were produced. Not wanting anyone to feel that same frustration, Forbes mastered the art of pitching and now provides a platform with Forbes Riley Studios, her television studio that introduces new products to the market.

Forbes has mastered the art of storytelling to communicate and spread the ideas she wants others to adopt. She believes that some of the things she has wanted so badly in her life didn't work out just so she could share the lessons she learned as a result. What a beautiful way to give disappointment a useful purpose.

Getting to the heart of your dreams and motivations and speaking them out loud is a favored practice for Forbes. The universe wants you to be very clear. There is no talking about Plan B. If you have a Plan B, the universe gets confused and may not deliver your big dream.

Forbes believes you are the sum of the things that happen to you. She seizes opportunities as they emerge and uses a vision board to remind her of the opportunities she hasn't encountered yet. Her realized dreams become great stories to tell and an amazing way to influence people. She dreams big and doesn't let fear hold her back. She knows she will land on her feet and has the tools and support to start something new should things not work out.

Forbes believes that personal truth begins and ends with you. No one can tell you what you are or are not. She urges you to be true to who you are because not everyone will see your vision exactly as you do - something to keep in mind as you embark on confident entrepreneurism.

The POWER Process

No one ever said life would be easy. Spoken Word Poet Sarah Kay summed it up well: *"This life will hit you hard, in the face, wait for you to get back up just so it can kick you in the stomach, but getting the wind knocked out of you is the only way to remind your lungs how much they like the taste of air."*

I have been in each one of those stages she describes. It was when I wasn't sure I would be able to get back up to taste air that the POWER process was born.

In my first book, *You Had It All Along*, I described each part of the acronym POWER as a key to unlocking Confidence at your Core. The POWER process is the beginning of building your personal confidence and skill set so you are ready for the connection, risk-taking, and authenticity that modern day entrepreneurship demands. Even if you want to, you can only compartmentalize your personal life from your professional one for so long. Inevitably, your personal life shows up. You get to decide how your personal and professional lives intersect and the 5 keys of POWER will help you along the way.

Key #1: <u>P</u>ersonal inventory

You need to understand who you are and your value before you can own it. A personal inventory is a deep dive to learn who you are. Be clear about what is important to you - your hopes and dreams, your skills, and your strengths and weaknesses. This should happen at a core level and on a business level, as it will form the basis for your messaging later on. Some people choose to take assessments for personality types or you can check out the activities I provided in *You Had It All Along.*

Bert Martinez made an interesting observation on taking a personal inventory. He has learned that everything an entrepreneur wants to accomplish will take twice as long and require ten times more effort than originally planned. Knowing your resources and resourcefulness greatly reduces the time and effort you might need. Completing a personal inventory identifies what you have and what you need to ask for, and it's vital for making progress.

Keep a record of your observations to use when you aren't feeling your best or you question your path of entrepreneurism. Pull out your personal inventory and review the evidence of why you are who you are and how much you have going for you. Confidence doesn't mean freedom from insecurity and fear. It does mean that you can identify what the current deficiency is and open your tool chest of skills and strategies to correct it.

This key is where the heart of your messaging will emerge. This will help you identify who you are as an entrepreneur and what you want to do. Without the completion of this key, which provides clarity, your success will be marginal at best. The clearer you are about what you can offer and how you want to show up in the marketplace, the better.

Remember if you don't know what your message is, no one else will either. It is difficult to connect with someone who is muddy about what they bring to the relationship. Every success hinges on a thorough completion of this key.

Key #2: <u>O</u>pen communication

In a broad sense, this involves examining how you communicate with yourself and others. This key is crucial to how you express your value and how you receive the value expressed by others. It also involves asking yourself these questions:

How do you receive messages and listen? Deepening your listening skills is one of the most effective ways to build your business.

How do you send messages? This is vital for business messaging and branding, copy writing, and other business communications. If marketing is viewed as an invitation to build a relationship, then how you extend the invitation is directly correlated to the relationship and connection you make.

Does your infrastructure and client care communicate that your clients are valued? Lack of clear policies and follow-up practices communicate much about how you value your clients. Pay attention to how you communicate expectations, desires, and vulnerability as well. Communicate the gift you have to give in a way that's attractive and appealing to others. Remember to consider body language, tone of voice, eye contact, hand shake, and attire.

Key #3: <u>W</u>ell-drawn boundaries

Let us begin with boundaries in your personal life. Be honest in answering:

- How effective are you in setting boundaries with yourself?

- Are you maintaining a healthy lifestyle?

- Can you turn off the negative self-talk that can cause a downward spiral of fear and self-doubt?

- Do you honor your desires and dreams or do the opinions of others drag you down?

- Do you demonstrate care when you communicate your expectations and when they are not being met?

The most abusive relationship you will ever have is with yourself. Setting boundaries raises your level of respect and the value you bring to the world, which is so vital when you connect with others. People might meet you where you are, but the reality is that they will usually meet your level of self-respect halfway. In case you need to hear it another way, think of a line graph from 1 to 10.

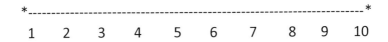

```
*------------------------------------------------------------------*
  1    2    3    4    5    6    7    8    9    10
```

Let's say your level of self-respect is an eight. If most people will meet you halfway, that puts their level of respect for you at a 4 – certainly not acceptable.

Without boundaries, it's difficult to sustain and grow. It's important to start as you mean to continue. Once an expectation has been set, it's hard to set a new boundary.
This is the key that leads to scalability. Without the right boundaries in place, you could end up working 20-hour days, seven days a week with no end in sight. Effective boundary setting is crucial for sustainable success.

Boundaries show up in business when it comes to attracting clients too. Stick to serving your ideal clients and cut the others loose.

As you get more comfortable making decisions, you also will have an easier time meeting and enforcing deadlines. Many people miss deadlines not because they're too busy or unaware, but simply because if they miss a deadline, they don't have to make a decision. As your decision-making gets stronger, so will your ability to set and meet boundaries, or in this instance, deadlines.

Key #4: <u>E</u>nvironment

There's a direct relationship between your physical environment and emotional well-being. Often physical environment ranks dead last in our priorities. If you piecemeal together furniture and supplies until you make higher profits, you won't enjoy your work space and won't want to be in it. Your creativity and innovation will suffer, and you will feel less professional.

Environment matters and should contribute to your success, not detract from it. Imagine for a moment that you have an uncomfortable desk chair. You start tracking the amount of time you are unproductive because you are uncomfortable in your chair. It totals 2 hours a day that your focus is on things other than bringing in new clients or creative new revenue streams. Let's say that you bill at $100 an hour. That is $200 a day, or $1000 a week or $4000 a month or $48,000 a year that you are potentially losing because you do not want to invest in a chair that feels good.

The equipment you use should fill your needs. If it is not, make a list of areas that you can improve and one by one acquire them as time and resources become available. Why let money escape you when you don't have to?

Be sure to look beyond your physical space to those you surround yourself with. That adage that you're the sum of the five people that you spend the most time with is true. Surround yourself with like-minded, supportive, ambitious, risk-takers who look at the world as an opportunity waiting for them.

Key #5: <u>R</u>eframing choices

Each time you choose, frame it to serve you and your goals most effectively. Choice is empowering and implies abundance.

It helps you define who you are in your business and outside of it. Refuse to fixate on your weaknesses or be defined by them. Reframing choices relegates power back to where it belongs ... in your hands.

One day, I had a client who rushed into my studio, threw her keys on the table, and declared, "I'm sorry I'm late. I'm a terrible time manager." I asked her if she liked how that defined her and if she could think of another way to reframe her weakness. She responded with a choice: "I've chosen not to manage my time well yet." Bingo! She got it – and the feeling of power that accompanies the act of reframing.

You may or may not have noticed the zebra stripes on the cover of this book. That was deliberate. It is part of my branding. Zebra print is a visual reminder that I have the power to choose. Wait! What? What in the world does zebra print have to do with the power to choose?

A few years ago as I was starting my coaching practice, I found myself in a desperate situation personally and stuck 'between a rock and a hard place'. I remember saying to a friend of mine that I had no choices. He encouraged me to think of the choices I had available, reminding me that I always have a choice. I made some different choices and learned that **I can't always choose myself out of a situation, but I always get to choose my reaction.** That truth is the most profound AND empowering realization I have made yet.

So what does that have to do with the zebra? A few months after that situation, I read a poem by Shel Silverstein called "Zebra Question". In it the poet asked the zebra if "he was black with white stripes or white with black stripes?" The zebra answered with questions of his own such as "Are you good with bad habits or bad with good habits? Are you noisy in a quiet world or quiet in a noisy world?" It went on but you get the picture.

Now whenever I see zebra print, it reminds me that I have the power to choose. Zebra print is a great visual reminder that communicates my core value to my audience. It all began when I made a choice to react and respond differently to a threatening situation that ended up empowering me rather than overcoming me.

Spotlight: Sarah Newton

Without Sarah Newton, the POWER Process would probably not exist. I hired Sarah to be my coach when I was a youth coach. I wanted to learn from the best and Sarah fit the bill. It was under her direction that I clarified the process of how I built confidence.

Sarah wasn't always an entrepreneur. She began as a police officer working with juvenile offenders in the United Kingdom. She became frustrated with how many youth were repeat offenders. She began questioning if there might be a better way to rehabilitate these juvenile offenders.

She came to know one of the youth because he kept being filtered through the system repeatedly. This young man, who was just doing what he could to survive, killed himself in his cell. His death had a profound impact on Sarah and inspired her to create the coaching practice that she currently has.

Shortly after this young man's death, she posed the question about how the police force was going to meet the needs of these kids, because what they were doing wasn't working. Dissatisfied with the answer, Sarah took a sabbatical to figure out the best course of action. Through study, introspection, creativity, innovation, and a whole lot of courage, she created Sarah Newton Consultancy. Sarah now works with youth every day. She has built an amazing practice and is touted as one of the leading youth authorities in the world. She has grown fond of disrupting social norms and inspiring people to think differently.

Sarah admitted she doesn't always feel confident, but she certainly practices like a confident entrepreneur. She rarely knows how she will accomplish a goal but she sets them anyway. She isn't always certain about the path to reach more youth, but says yes anyway. She listens to the call and does what she can to make it happen.

Her time in the police force taught her many skills that have aided her as an entrepreneur. She saw tragedy that would break her heart, but that didn't stop her from doing her job. She learned tenacity, perseverance, courage, and resilience. Her career in the force also helps put some of the decisions she makes into perspective. When you have experienced the tragedy of young lives being wasted, it puts choosing which advertising genre to employ into perspective.

Sarah is an awesome example of the sweet spot of entrepreneurship. She completes daily check-ins to make sure her mindset and energy are in proper order. She works on her connections, continually trying to find new meaningful ways to engage or serve them. She doesn't allow naysayers to sideline her. She adheres to the wisdom of Winston Churchill: "**You will never reach your destination if you stop and throw stones at every dog that barks.**" Sarah also uses solid structural practices like not ending the day until she has completed three moneymaking activities.

Sarah's best advice: Don't get caught up in the Imposter Syndrome. Don't question why people would listen to you and feel inadequate or like you may not know enough. To combat this, she suggests you list the top five reasons you should do what you do and answer why you are the perfect person to do it. You are more qualified than you know. Remember, confident entrepreneurs say yes and trust they will have everything they need to get the job done.

Part II: The Sweet Spot

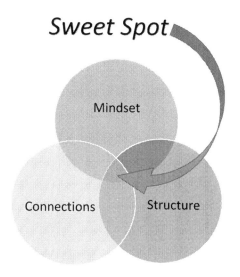

If your goal is to build a platform for sharing and engagement, it's worth knowing the pieces that need to intersect. I've boiled it down to three areas I call the "sweet spot," but each piece has a litany of practices used to create it.

*The big three are **Mindset, Connections** and **Structure**. As you work to align these three areas, you will begin to see the rewards of confident entrepreneurship. The entrepreneurs described in this book had these three pieces in common.*

Now let's dive into the sweet spot so you can fully benefit as well.

Choices to Changes

Mindset Moxie

Organizing your thoughts sounds like a logical, practical practice, and it can be for the thoughts that you're actually aware of. It's the 70,000 subconscious thoughts that cause most of the disorder. It's even harder when the challenge appears to be intangible. Let's take a look at what makes up your mindset and some of the reasons you end up thinking and feeling the way you do.

I used the word *moxie* to describe the mindset a confident entrepreneur needs to use. Moxie is defined as the *ability to be active; to have courage or determination.* Without moxie, your mindset can be the most paralyzing aspect of entrepreneurship.

Maybe you aren't exactly full of moxie. That happens especially with those confused entrepreneurs mentioned earlier. With risk-taking comes self-sabotage, fear, resistance to change, scarcity, confusion, and challenges. You need to manage your mindset to create the space to develop trust that you will be supported in all situations.

So let's look at those mindset issues and the best ways to manage them when they arise.

1. Fear

First, recognize that there's a difference between fear and danger.

Danger is when five large people are coming towards you with weapons with the intent to hurt you. Danger is when you're locked in a car that's sinking in a lake. Danger is when you're moving a refrigerator and it falls over, pinning you to the ground.

Fear is a little different. Fear is a mental construct that exists to keep you safe in what you know. It prevents you from straying too far out of your comfort zone, regardless of how detrimental the comfort zone may be. You fear discomfort, insecurity, and uncertainty, particularly when it comes to outcomes. You fear being vulnerable and exposing your weaknesses to the judgement of others. You fear not connecting and being rejected. You fear making mistakes and experiencing failure. You even fear success that may require you to leap out of a comfort zone that keep you feeling small.

That can be an awful lot of fear going on and sometimes it's present all at once. Imagine what would happen if you channeled the energy consumed by fear into courage. The path to confidence begins where your fear lives, but you travel through courage to reach your final destination.

Your body reacts to fear and danger in the same way. Your body's job is to keep you safe. That's why adrenaline flows when you perceive danger. It provides the added energy you may need to remove yourself from the dangerous situation.

When you feel fear, your body may react in the same way. It wants to keep you safe. Coping mechanisms show up, such as negative voices and even physiological ailments that keep you protected and feeling safe within your comfort zone.

Wouldn't it be great if the body could discern fear from danger? While we have to live with what we have, it is possible to dismiss fear and your body's response to it once you identify what the feeling is.

Confidence is often defined as the absence of fear, but that's not totally accurate. You can walk through fear to courage and on to confidence. Dr. Brene Brown declares that **"You can't get to courage without walking through vulnerability."**

Vulnerability results from exposing something about yourself and leaving yourself open to being judged. A confident entrepreneur uses fear like this:

You feel uncomfortable or insecure. → **FEAR**

You define the fear and become vulnerable → **DEFINE**

You examine what you fear and decide if the new outcome is more important that the idea of staying safe. → **DEFY**

You do something different, whether it's making a decision, changing a behavior, learning a new skill, or stretching beyond your comfort zone. This is the action or implementation phase. → **DO**

When you realize that the outcome, although uncomfortable, is satisfying fear melts away and you are inspired to continue this change of thought or behavior. Knowing that you have been supported through this journey creates the evidence you need to step into → **CONFIDENCE**

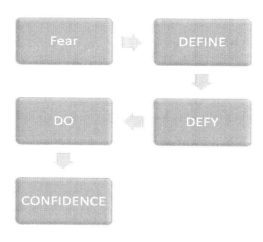

Notice that three of the phases of achieving confidence involve making choices:

- You choose to define and expose your vulnerability.

- You choose to confront fear and defy it.

- You choose to act or think courageously to provide a platform for confidence.

You won't be confident if you don't trust your ability to make decisions. Without trust, you send a signal that you don't believe that you will be fully supported regardless of the outcome.

When you are struggling with fear, it is a great idea to identify where you are on the path. That knowledge will facilitate quicker movement along the way to get you to feeling and practicing confidently.

2. Resistance to change

Your choices lead to changes. Even positive change is uncomfortable. Anytime you stretch from what you know it is a change. Your willingness to embrace the accompanying discomfort dictates to what degree you will resist. Resistance to change is often the number 2 killer of confidence.

When you're making a transition, it's in your best interest to notice what you think, how you feel, and what happens in your body. Being aware in this way allows you to see the patterns - a vital key to understanding which pieces can change and to what degree.

This bodily awareness can be helpful not only for you personally, but also as you facilitate change for others. Noticing how others are experiencing resistance and what the patterns of fear create in them will be valuable in knowing how to assist them through transition. **As an entrepreneur, you are a change agent.** When you are confident that you can help others achieve lasting change, then you all win.

Most people get excited about making change for a minute until they realize the tremendous amounts of change that can happen. Then the idea of change becomes so daunting that they stop before they even get started.

As an entrepreneur, your job is to ask people to change the way they think, feel or behave. When you approach your audience as the primary resource for them to overcome their resistance to change, you create a loyal client base. When you speak their language, understand their challenges, and share strategies and solutions to ease the transition, you create loyal clients who know, like, and trust you. Selling conversations become obsolete because you provide value, act as a change agent, and prove to people that they can work with you. It becomes a much easier *yes* when you understand the role you need to play.

3. Self-esteem

Confident entrepreneurship is much easier with positive self-esteem. This means you believe you are worthy of the support showing up.

Challenges arise when you aren't sure of your worth. You might question if you're the right person for the job. You could believe you won't have the resources to support you because you aren't worthy of them. You may feel you haven't proven your value or even miscomprehend how much value you provide.

This web of insecurity acts like the grim reaper on our confidence. Without belief in your worth, value, and capabilities, confidence will not have a fertile ground to breed. You will remain in a wasteland of confusion and darkness where your ability to serve and contribute to the betterment of society will be seriously limited.

4. Indecision

This is such an issue for many people. There are two reasons that people are indecisive:

- They don't trust their own judgment. They learned to second-guess their judgment, usually because an outcome was unpleasant or uncomfortable from the past.

- They fear the outcome (negative or positive). Fear causes discomfort in decision-making, even when it appears to protect you and keep you safe.

If risk-taking is the hallmark of successful entrepreneurs, indecision is a constant and direct challenge. Confident entrepreneurs recognize that the payoff is bigger than the discomfort of achieving it.

So the question becomes how do you get comfortable with taking risks. Here are a few suggestions:

1. **Learn to trust your own judgment.** You may not always like the outcomes of your decisions, but you survived them and actually grew stronger and wiser because of them. Surrender the desire to be absolutely certain of an outcome and proceed with faith that the support you need will emerge.

2. **Create a plan.** It's easy to try to accomplish too much at one time. Take that big goal and create a series of actions that will help you reach it. Eat the elephant one bite at a time. Making incremental changes virtually assures success. If it still feels overwhelming, break down the goal even smaller.

3. **Celebrate.** When you're trying to eliminate indecision and encourage risk-taking, celebrating making any choice is important, regardless of the outcome. You'll learn more about the art of celebrating and why it is so important later. Positive reinforcement of a desired action creates a pleasure pathway in your brain that connects the action to the desired response.

4. **View all outcomes as gifts.** If you can shift the outcome to a learning experience rather than a judged positive or negative outcome, you will have much more freedom to act. If you perceive a benefit regardless of the outcome, fear of success or failure dissolves. Each of the confident entrepreneurs featured here were as quick to embrace failure as they were success. They understood that there is as much to gain from failing as there is succeeding.

If you believe that you will be supported in all you do and act accordingly, risk-taking becomes accessible and welcomed. You develop very different relationships with risk-taking and it benefits you positively. If you view each outcome as a learning event, you will seek opportunities that are available rather than remaining stuck in fear of making wrong decisions.

Confidence does not encourage imprudence, and due diligence is surely required. Confidence is more about the time you afford the due diligence before taking action. Inactivity can be detrimental to entrepreneurs and confidence may be all you need to reach the tipping point for successful risk-taking.

Risk-taking influences our ability to connect with others. If the risk of vulnerability or relationship building is too high, true connection will be elusive. Without connection, entrepreneurial dreams will be difficult if not impossible to acquire.

5. Belief

Belief is tricky because what comes out of your mouth may be different than what goes on in your head. When you say you believe, you need to be all in – body, mind, and soul; otherwise, you'll send mixed signals. Just as consumers won't buy when they're confused, when your thoughts, actions, and intentions don't support your idea, it will not materialize. Get real about how much you believe in your idea/offering/message and work hard to overcome the obstacles that hinder your beliefs from materializing.

Suppose you want to earn $5000 this month and think you *believe* that it can happen. Once you say it, you may immediately ask what will happen if you don't and then start listing the reasons why it probably won't. In this case you're clearly more grounded in disbelief than belief. You're actually inviting those thoughts of disbelief to materialize. Your vocabulary, tone of voice, and actions must align with your belief in order to materialize your thoughts positively.

Act like what you want is already a reality. You'll invest in what will make your dream a reality if you already believe it has been ordered. This contributes to an abundant mindset. Go ahead and create action around what you believe to offer a unified intention.

6. Scarcity vs. abundance

Scarcity is another confidence killer. When you don't believe you have enough, you invite lack into your life. This thought pattern appears particularly when you view your competition and assume there isn't enough business to go around. What's vital to realize is that you have no competition. No one is going to conduct business, practice entrepreneurship, build relationships or deliver resources exactly like you are. When you step out of the fear of there not being enough resources (i.e., clients, customers or audience), you step into abundance.

Other entrepreneurs may offer the same product in the same industry as you, but that doesn't mean there's not enough business to go around.

The most successful entrepreneurs are *collaborators,* not competitors.

When your mindset is stuck in how to get an edge over your competition, you're using your energy in a destructive and scarcity-inviting activity. When you act like there's a lack or scarcity, that's what you attract. Is that what you really want?

Of course, the act of gratitude is an act of abundance. When you're grateful for what you possess and signal that it is enough, abundance takes place. Adopting attitudes of gratitude and keeping gratitude journals are great practices. Abundance attracts abundance. Why not invite more?

7. Mindfulness

Practicing mindfulness is another practice of abundance. If you stop waiting for what might come and enjoy what is already here, you attract more of that fullness into your life. If you do your best with what you have right now, you confirm abundance. You will miss opportunities in the present moment if your eyes are fixed on what you want, rather than what you already have.

Another avenue for inviting lack is patience. But wait, isn't that a virtue? Although the way you behave while you wait is a virtue, the act of waiting implies that what you have now is not enough. As abundance invites abundance, lack invites lack.

Please don't misunderstand. It's important to set goals and achieve them. It's vital to want more, bigger, and better because it provides the initiative that makes action a reality. The challenge lies in waiting patiently, expecting to catch a break rather than acting mindfully by achieving what you can now. That may mean taking many small steps towards a goal as opposed to waiting for that one big leap that may never come. It's about doing your best with what you have to bring you closer to achieving your goal.

8. Clarity

This is so important. Stagnation, confusion, and loss of focus set in when lack of clear purpose occurs. Rather than forward motion and growth, there is rarely any movement. Confusion breeds less engagement, less relationship building and less financial return.

Clarity is vital both on an entrepreneurial and personal level. Knowing why you feel the way you feel and do what you do is critical in identifying your values and courses of action. Do the work to get clear. Having clarity is one of the most confidence-inducing practices you can engage in.

9. Focus

Less confident entrepreneurs are cautious. They do relentless research. They analyze. They evaluate. They research some more. They explore other options. They create strategic plans.

You may be thinking that isn't so bad. It sounds like they are getting all of their ducks in a row before they pull the trigger. That becomes precisely the problem. They rarely pull the trigger for action.

I can't tell you how many planning sessions, content calendars and mind maps I created with the intent for inspired action. Funny how they seem to have been a waste of time because very little action occurred from all of that labor.

Keefe Duterte shared an awesome quote that fits so perfectly here: **"Action expresses priority".** If growth is your priority, you will engage in activities that promote growth. If you hesitate, wait and only plan, your priority is honoring fear and safety. If your priority is serving your clients, you're going to create a kick-ass client experience. If your priority is only to make money, your actions will reflect that and your ability to connect and build relationships will suffer.

Confident entrepreneurs absolutely do their due diligence, but they also do not fear acting on it. Why should they? They trust that they will be supported regardless of the outcome.

Spotlight: Keefe Duterte

Keefe Duterte didn't always have the mindset moxie needed to practice as a confident entrepreneur, but he worked at it until he did. He didn't stop when he hit the sweet spot. He continually is searching and learning how to practice in the most efficient and courageous ways available. His influence as an entrepreneur is encouraging and inspiring.

Keefe Duterte now heads a successful insurance agency, but he didn't start out that way. Originally, Keefe began as a wealth manager for Merrill Lynch. He was working 80-100 hours a week and making great money, but he paid a high price in the time he sacrificed being away from his family.

Keefe entered entrepreneurship after consulting with one of his clients – one who owned insurance agencies and seemed to have an abundance of time and money. Keefe wanted that freedom for himself. His family time was suffering tremendously and it was a sacrifice he no longer wanted to make.

He confidently jumped into entrepreneurship and quickly learned that being an entrepreneur can be one of the loneliest positions on the planet. His agencies did well for a time, but Keefe's lack of entrepreneurial and management skills nearly bankrupted the company. He was going to crash and burn if he didn't do something to course-correct soon.

Although Keefe originally let ego stand in the way of asking for help, he eventually looked to coaches and mentors. An avid reader and quote collector, he also sought the wisdom of words and ideas. Keefe surrounded himself with people who were having more success than he was which turned out to be a worthy investment of his time, effort, and money. He not only turned around the company, but it is now recognized as the top 3% of all agencies in the country. Through his interactions and connections, he learned the entrepreneurial, management, and personal skills he needed to not only make money but create a healthy work-life balance.

To help others achieve the success and balance he found, Keefe collaborated with like-minded individuals to form Agency Sales Academy, which teaches success skills to other agency owners. They use the acronym HERO to share skills with their participants: **H**iring the right people, creating the right **E**nvironment, **R**evenue management, and **O**perations. Doesn't that sound a whole lot like the sweet spot of confident entrepreneurism?

Time is especially important to Keefe. He has learned to be relentless about his boundaries, whether it's his morning ritual of getting grounded and connecting to his motivators and goals before his family gets up, or saying no to bright shiny projects. The most important measure of success for Keefe is the time he spends with his family and the way he encourages others. He believes that **LOVE** is spelled **T-I-M-E**. What a different world we would live in if we all paid attention to that.

Keefe is convinced that it's important to affirm who you are every day. He suggests using daily affirmations such as those from Og Mandino ("I will persist until I succeed") or Mohammed Ali ("Suffer now and live the rest of your life like a champion). Confident entrepreneurship is not always easy, but Keefe so beautifully demonstrates that when you find the sweet spot, success – however you define it – can absolutely be achieved.

Courageous Connections

Entrepreneurship is no longer only about commerce. It's now about connection.

As a people, we no longer want to be treated as a commodity or valued only by our spending power. We want to be seen as individuals with value beyond our income. Entrepreneurs who want to be successful are connectors, not salespeople. If you don't have the confidence in your ability to connect with others, entrepreneurial success will be elusive or fleeting at best.

The era of viewing consumers as dollar signs is over. They are demanding that you see beyond their spending power if you want to receive their money.

For some entrepreneurs, the vulnerability of connection is far more risky than anything they have ever done and it will be too high a price to pay for success. Those are not true entrepreneurs. They may aspire to be, but in refusing to fill a need, they lack the true nature of entrepreneurism. The entrepreneur with the courage and the confidence to connect will lead the pack over and over again. Their sphere of influence grows in direct relation to their ability to connect with more (and the right) people.

Connection is different from reach. Reach means that someone hears about you and your offering. Connection means they're willing to buy from you. Why? Because you have demonstrated your value to the consumer's life. This goes way beyond a slick sales page or ad in a newspaper. It is about entering into a relationship.

Consumers no longer want you to exploit their vulnerabilities without exposing some of your own.

An entrepreneur must be vulnerable and demonstrate the courage of connection for the relationship to work for both sides.

That is risky business – far riskier than losing money. Those who are willing to put themselves, their values, and their money on the line become magnets for success. They exude confidence that makes them incredibly captivating, and they will naturally draw a following.

Confidence in connection is:

- Faith or trust that you will be stronger than the vulnerabilities you expose. It is the unshakable belief that you will be supported even when you aren't sure how.

- Taking a leap of faith by sharing your value and who you are, knowing that what you share is more important than avoiding the discomfort of sharing it.

- Your willingness to be uncomfortable while you ask someone else to do the same.

With every connection and every transaction, you are asking someone to make a choice. Choose to connect. Choose to see the value of what you offer. Choose to allow changes in your life from each transaction and connection.

Change is so difficult for most people. Asking people to change the way they think, feel or behave is risky. The percentage of successful integration of change for most is low. That's why self-help is a booming industry. People believe that they can change by deciding to read a book or listen to a speaker, but it requires much more investment than that. It requires activity.

Change is not static. By leading the consumer through the change cycle and exposing your own weaknesses through that cycle, you will be more successful. You become connected to the process. You're no longer separate from those you serve. In an era when so many people feel alone, invisible, and unheard, providing the chance to connect is huge. It creates trust and loyalty - the perfect storm for meeting the needs of both parties.

Ready to make connections a bit easier? Keep these things in mind.

1. Be authentic

Covering up your flaws and imperfections creates an environment that doesn't foster creativity or innovation. You will waste so much energy trying to maintain an unrealistic, perfect façade that your health may suffer, your relationships may suffer and you will be exhausted.

As you unshackle yourself from the illusion that you are perfect, you will notice more abundance. When you are real about fears and doubts, they seem to melt away. It is almost as if they cannot survive the attention. When you allow others to really see you, warts and all, real connections take place. Sure being authentic will turn away some people, but for most others it can even be a saving grace.

When you are yourself, you can put your energy into so much more. Show your personality, experience, and knowledge rather than creating a persona you think people will be attracted to - this is a key practice in confident entrepreneurship. Don't worry about attracting everyone – you aren't supposed to.

2. Embrace vulnerability

Confident people ask for help. First it is important to identify what you need, which can put you in a very vulnerable place. Exposing yourself and your needs can be risky, but **risk-taking is the hallmark of confident entrepreneurship**.

Remember, being vulnerable is the second stage in the path from fear into confidence and with good reason. Your journey along this path into confident living depends on it.

Asking for what you need shouldn't be that difficult, but many people struggle with it. Again, if you trust that you will be supported in each endeavor, dismiss the fear of asking and ASK! It is much more difficult and time consuming to wait for help to arrive. Be proactive and specific and ask for assistance. Facilitate the opportunity for resources to appear.

3. Associate with risk-takers

One of the best ways to get over the fear of risk-taking is to be around those who do it. Not only will you will learn how to take risks fearlessly; you'll also learn the tools to employ in getting there.

Being around risk-takers gives you the courage to participate in like activities. You'll learn how some risks pay off and others do not. You'll observe that survival happens either way, which will help remove some of your fear and anxiety.

4. Collaborate

As Scott Stratten of *UnMarketing* fame says, **"If you are your authentic self, you have no competition."** No one offers exactly what you do.

If you feel the need, learn what your perceived competition is doing. Be aware that this is a defining point of confidence. Your goal should be to feel so confident in your essence– your systems, your ability to connect and build relationships, your customer care and product development - what anyone else does is irrelevant.

Your performance and offerings should be enough without tearing apart your perceived competition. Why waste energy trying to beat out those in a similar industry? Wouldn't you rather spend your energy creating brilliance that will catapult you in stature and reputation in the eyes of those you serve?

Competition is part of a scarcity vs. abundance mindset. Competing creates scarcity. There is more than enough business for any one entrepreneur to handle.

You can't work with everyone. Not everyone will be a good fit for you. Choose to work with or influence the people you are meant to. That's what confidence is all about, right? It's so much better to work with your ideal set of clients than contribute to the mindset of lack.

Combat the competitive/scarcity mindset with **collaboration**. Work with people on promoting each other – even when you are in the same industry. By supporting others, you bring attention not only to them but also to yourself.

Confident entrepreneurs want to create a reputation of service, authenticity, integrity, and collaboration. By collaborating, they widen their sphere of influence, amplify their reputation, create a climate of service, and foster a sense of community. That is a total win for all involved!

Spotlight: Joie Gharrity

Joie Gharrity has a natural flair for helping others shine brilliantly. Partly from her background and training, but partly because she radiates confidence. Ever mindful of her sweet spot - the organization of her mindset, connections and structure - Joie has become a tremendous example for entrepreneurs to follow.

Joie Gharrity's entrance into entrepreneurship as a brand strategist at No. 113 Branding was via Hollywood. She found out right away that being an entrepreneur is much different than working for the machine of a large studio. Even if you offer the same skill set, it really is a completely different animal when you go it alone and you no longer have billions of dollars worth of influence backing you.

Joie spent her first year as an entrepreneur feeling lonely and unsupported because she did not belong to a tribe. She did not have systems and structures in place. Being a creative, she was continually reinventing the wheel with each client, and that rarely promotes growth - a common dilemma for many entrepreneurs who leave companies to strike out on their own. That exhausted her and she found that clients rarely promote and that impacted her business growth. The sweet spot sometimes takes a while to find, and Joie spent nearly a year away aligning practices of mindset, connections, and structure so she could be more fulfilled and successful as an entrepreneur.

In her time away, Joie got very clear about her *why* and what she was offering and how she could serve. She created not only business systems, but client systems that enabled them to easily bring life to their company brands. She has created some awesome strategies to build visibility - all born out of her personal discomfort with it. Uncomfortable being in front of the camera instead of behind it making others look good, Joie fights the desire to be less visible. She walks her talk and exemplifies the visibility strategies she asks the women entrepreneurs that are her clients to employ.

Joie Gharrity is all about building community and deep personal and business relationships. Her goal is to shine the spotlight on other entrepreneurs so their brilliance can shine front and center. Spotlighting other brands is a networking technique that Joie learned in the Hollywood entertainment industry. When you spotlight other brands, you will find the spotlight turning back on your brand. People support people that show support for them. This strategy works best when you lead from your heart and from a place of integrity.

Spotlighting another brand expands the net worth of both brands because it introduces the brands to each other's backyards. When you highlight someone else, it increases the size of everybody's backyard and brings attention to your brand in places you might not currently have it.

Joie uses multiple avenues of media to feature other business owners and increase their visibility. She has a virtual magazine, weekly happy hour spotlights, joint venture blog posts she calls the Double Dip (as highlighted in the Huffington Post), and a beautiful online Facebook Community that supports and encourages its members. She has made a practice of spotlighting others, and her success has followed in a big way. These practices have helped Joie to be OF service to others, not IN service, which is of vital importance to her.

Boundaries are an important part of Joie's practice. She is tenacious about her daily self-care rituals, especially meditation. It is too easy to get off track and not stay true to who you are. She worked in a difficult industry where opinions were considered truth. Establishing appropriate boundaries to receive feedback and know what to do with it was important to Joie's growth. She encourages others to protect themselves and their brand if others are criticizing it. You don't have to stay quiet or look the other way.

Another practice Joie wanted to share is to be authentic and true to who you are. Show up for you. When you show up, you can build a community. When you share your stories, it opens doors for others to connect with you and create space for them to share their stories. It is impossible to do it alone and it hinders growth when you try to be a lone wolf. Instead grow your tribe so that your company brand can soar.

Connect. Collaborate. Build community. It can be the lifeblood of entrepreneurship as Joie so beautifully demonstrates.

Savvy Structure

This part of the Sweet Spot trio is the most business oriented. Lack of structure is a major reason why entrepreneurs do not feel confident in their businesses.

If you haven't set up an infrastructure that supports your connections and mission, you won't feel confident moving forward and growing. Many begin their entrepreneurial pursuits with the bare minimum just to get started. This can make growth especially painful if structure is not in place. Not only will you need to learn how to serve more people; you'll have to learn the systems to support you.

1. Establish evergreen practices

Evergreen practices allow your business to continue running if you have to step away from your business. They are structured so that someone could walk in and either continue to run the business or shut it down. Many entrepreneurs *are* their service or product, so if you couldn't show up for work, the business would cease to function. If you set up evergreen practices, that may not be necessarily true.

Here are a few things you should consider documenting:

- Everyday procedures: accounting, marketing, client care, legal concerns, insurance coverage
- Company policies for all aspects of your business
- Lists of vendors/services with contact info and passwords
- Contracts or agreement templates

- Exit strategy upon your death
- Database of clients or customers
- Security procedures

"Going evergreen" also makes it more efficient when you bring on team members. Training them in company policies or procedures will be a snap because you've created a one-stop shop of all policies and procedures already.

2. Determine your needs

Identifying what your needs are – and updating the list regularly - is a great way to create strategies in getting your needs met. With a plan in place on how to meet your needs, they will be filled faster than without it. Nothing is off limits. Please consider your environment, supplies, equipment, location, team members, support, insurance, follow-up methods, marketing, and web services, just to name a few.

3. Develop a compensation plan

Although a compensation plan is mandatory, it doesn't have to be only monetary. You can barter services (which is why the needs assessment is important), find media partners, partner with affiliates, etc.

If you feel uncomfortable asking for money in exchange for your product or services, remember that to serve others, you need to take care of your basic needs first. If you're worried about your electricity being turned off, you aren't going to be present for your clients full throttle.

When your attention is divided, you may miss opportunities or provide less than stellar service or client care. That can be the death of a business. It is difficult to show up as confident entrepreneur when you're not sure how the rent will get paid this month.

4. Build a team

Whether you embrace this idea or not, you can't practice entrepreneurship all alone. There are only so many things you can do well.

Brooks Hoffos is a great example of this. He credits his team for all of his success. They are an extension of who he is. He built his team out of necessity and the team grows as his enterprises grow.

The FUSE Realty Development Team: Luana McDonald, Christie Clarke, Brooks Hoffos, Dale Williams, Clarence Wesloski, Tiara Doar, Ashley Carragher,

So why is it so important to build a team? Because no one is good at everything. You began your entrepreneurial journey because you felt strongly about what you have to offer the world. You didn't begin so you can run yourself ragged completing the daily tasks, the marketing, the accounting, and whatever your practice, product or service is.

There are people who are brilliant in things you don't do well or don't like to do. Let them shine in their fields so you can shine in yours. Imagine how much creative energy you could focus if you didn't have to complete the tasks that weigh you down?

Starting out, you most likely can't afford to hire or outsource work. One of your first objectives is to raise enough capital to hire help where you need it. It may seem frivolous but it isn't. Why are you doing a task you could outsource for $10 an hour when you could be doing something that will bring in much more revenue? It may sting a bit at first, but will be worth it in the end.

Hiring a team can be a daunting task if you're uncomfortable with leadership. Once you learn how to manage your team and inspire them to be brilliant, your business will grow almost immediately.

As you build your team, recall this quote from Liz Wiseman, the author of *Multipliers* "What is possible if you can access all of the intelligence in your organization? By extracting people's full capacity, multipliers get twice the capacity from them."

Imagine if you could inspire your team to be twice as productive and innovative! What would happen if you had more than just your brainpower and energy working towards growth? Tell me again why this is a step that many entrepreneurs want to avoid as long as possible.

Confidence helps when building a team, in no small part because it inspires confidence in you from your team members. Trust your gut and inspire your team to trust theirs. Lead by example. Grow alongside them rather than jump ahead of them. You will each grow into your own brilliance and the results will be phenomenal.

If you find yourself in a position that isn't the right fit, use your confidence and trust that you will be supported even in this situation. Hiring a team is an investment and a risk that occasionally may not yield the best results. Knowing that there is a gift, a lesson in the experience that makes the act less risky, and the investment is assured to pay off. The payoff may not always look like you expected, but some kind of payoff will emerge nonetheless. It is all about how you frame the experience.

5. Track your money

Attention to money breeds abundance.

If you're having a hard time making ends meet, start examining your money patterns to understand the lens you use to view money – scarcity or abundance. Notice the way you speak about money. How often do you say that you cannot do or purchase something because you can't afford it? That's clearly a lack mentality and you're inviting more of it.

How about reframing your money decisions as choices? Try saying "I am choosing not to spend my money on this" to see how it feels. Choice implies that you have something to choose from, and that indicates a measure of abundance. A simple shift of words can have a huge impact on what you're attracting into your life.

6. Balance feminine and masculine energy

This may be a little woo-woo for some people, but it has merit. Traditional feminine qualities include feeling and more abstract thinking led by intuition and creativity. Masculine energy tends to push until the task is complete. Thoughts are linear and logical and plans and strategies are created and executed.

Pay attention to the qualities that tip the scale. If you're always planning and pushing forward, you'll eventually hit the wall so hard that you will be forced to re-evaluate. Likewise, if you are a feeler and more abstract thinker, the work doesn't get done because it lacks forward energy.

Trusting that the resources will arrive means you get to be an active participant in attracting them to you. However, you have to do your part. Sitting at your desk and chanting "resources appear" is not the way they arrive. Being all in and doing what you can do is a vital part of the equation.

When I started practicing a more balanced approach, my business began to thrive. The combination of the energies has really helped me succeed at a regular and consistent pace. Honor yourself and know your limits. As Karen McMillan says, give yourself permission to "slow down so you can speed up." Achieving balance helps create entrepreneurial success rather than burnout.

7. Seek feedback

This is crucial especially if you're a solopreneur. You have limited vision, and there are things you don't or can't see.

There is power in collective minds.

Be careful when asking for feedback and ask only those you trust and have a qualified opinion. You must trust that they will not be butt-kissers or abusers and will give you honest feedback to help you grow. Such people do not have to be many in number, but they need to be reliable and trustworthy.

There's also a difference between asking for feedback and receiving it. Be gracious and open-minded when you ask for it. If you're looking to hear only what you want to hear, don't bother asking. Learn the difference between qualified feedback and opinions. Qualified feedback is derived from your target market or those experienced in your field and is the only type worthy of your time and attention.

You'll also get unsolicited feedback just because you're putting yourself out there. You'll hear from haters, naysayers, and those who are jealous or mean-spirited. Some may say "Yes!" to everything you do for the sake of personal gain. Feedback can be both useful and toxic. Learn to tell the difference.

When discerning the quality of feedback and what you want to do with it, keep these questions in mind:

1.   Is it real?

2.   Is it true?

3.   Is this how you want to be defined?

4.   Does this serve you well?

5.   Is there anything you would or could do differently that would help keep you in line with your values?

Spotlight: Brooks Hoffos

Brooks Hoffos is by far the most humble entrepreneur you will ever meet. He's uncomfortable talking about himself and almost declined the interview for this book. He feared that most people associate confidence with ego and he clearly is all about his team and not his ego.

Brooks is a very successful entrepreneur but attributes his success not to himself, but to the people he surrounds himself with. Brooks is a great example of learning well beyond the classroom and squeezing every lesson he can out of his experiences, contributing to his immense growth. He is incredibly successful today as the owner of multiple businesses including his passion: FUSE Realty Development.

School was not a place that bred confidence or self-esteem for the young Brooks Hoffos. A bout with spinal meningitis as a boy left him in a coma for months, and his parents were told he would be in a vegetative state the rest of his life. He was paralyzed for a long time after regaining consciousness, but eventually regained all that he lost except one thing. As a result of his illness, his brain rewired itself, reorganizing his reading, writing, and thought patterns into what is defined today as dyslexia.

It's inspiring to observe Brooks and see how he thrives in the face of chaotic situations that would bring many to their knees. He is happiest when he can problem-solve and sees challenges as opportunities for growth and learning. It is his tenacity and openness to working with his team that contributes to the success he enjoys today.

Although Brooks is a master at team building, he is also a master connector. The care he takes with others to help them grow and treating them like he would want to be treated, shines through in every interaction. His customer care model and interaction with his team and clients are nothing short of brilliant. Always mindful and present in each moment, Brooks draws out the stories that everyone has to tell.

His favorite way to solve a challenge is to get to know the people he is working with to find their motivators and then create solutions that will work for everyone. He draws on the strengths of others as revealed by their history to discover acceptable solutions for the present.

Not surprisingly, the key to POWER that most impacted Brooks was taking a personal inventory. He urges you to find out who you are. Be happy and love yourself – the good and the bad. **Your moments of fear and insecurity are not negative, but opportunities to change and grow**. Surround yourself with those whose input is valuable not just because they love you, but because they drive you to be your best self.

Part III: Sharpening Your Edge

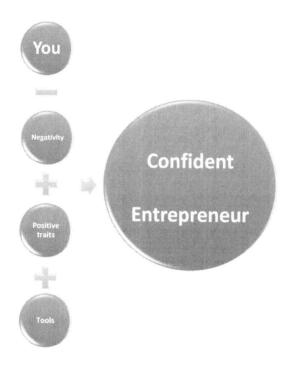

Keeping an edge sharp requires tools. This part of the book examines some of the tools, traits and processes that produce the most effective organization of mindset, connections and structure.

Some of the following are things that must be let go. Others will fill the empty space that subtraction opens. The rest are tools to use all along the way to enhance your practice of confidence.

Choices to Changes

Subtracting to Add

To embrace your own power and success, you'll probably need to open up the space for the new skills and perspectives you'll be adding. The following traits can be protectors and coping mechanisms when survival is your only goal. Those that want to grow will be chained to the status quo as long as these are a part of the scenery.

1. Perfectionism

This is something that many entrepreneurs struggle with and it's understandable. Appearances matter, and if you don't appear to have your act together, who will do business with you? There will be times in your business that feeding the positive perception of who you are, how busy you are, and how you look and behave will appear more important than the service you render.

This kind of thinking sets you up for trouble. When you are preoccupied with the impossible illusion of perfection, your focus and energy are removed from what truly will inspire growth for your business. As discussed in Courageous Connections, authenticity and allowing for vulnerability are vital to making connections that count. It is so difficult to rebound when reality does not jive with the appearances you portray. It creates an atmosphere of distrust and that is an outcome you definitely do not want.

Perfectionism stems from fishbowl living. The day you signed up as an entrepreneur, you agreed to a certain degree of this. You'll be subject to public scrutiny and judgment that can impact you personally and economically. If you aren't careful, it could cause your business to collapse.

2. Complacency

It's so easy to let things slide, turn a blind eye and burying your head in the sand so you don't have to face reality. Coasting along without addressing deficiencies can hurt you professionally and personally.

It's tempting to ignore things that don't feel great, but don't. This can lead to a whole host of problems that could be avoided if you're paying attention.

Complacency is such a passive activity that it's easy to counteract. Be courageous enough to hold the mirror up, get out the magnifying glass, and dive into what could be hurting you. You will be supported in your need.

3. Ignorance

Ignorance is bliss only until you get smacked in the gut with it. This goes hand in hand with complacency. You can only use the excuse that you *did not know* for so long. We have too many resources literally at our fingertips to feign ignorance.

Get educated. Take advantage of seminars, workshops, conferences, webinars, websites and books to increase your knowledge. Find mentors and coaches who can help you. When you have an encyclopedia on your phone, it is really hard to use ignorance as an excuse for not growing.

102

4. Negative judgment

Oh boy! This is a doozie! Giving up negative judgment on yourself – both personally and professionally – is a tough challenge. Negative judgment can result in guilt, inadequacy, shame, frustration, jealousy, confusion, stagnation, and more. None of those is terribly productive when trying to grow a business.

Negative judgment keeps you small and limits possibilities. It signals that you do not trust that you will be supported, plus it kills confidence and self-esteem. Trouble starts when you compare yourself to others. Keep your eyes on your path and not anyone else's.

5. Clutter

Clutter can permeate our thoughts, environment, and relationships. Clean it up. Let it go!

Letting go of clutter is difficult, but it will feel like cutting away a thousand-pound noose from your neck. You miss things in a disordered environment because that very disorder invites you to get complacent. You might just stack the mail in a pile and address it later. Your organizational system doesn't have to rival Martha Stewart's, but it deserves your attention - sooner rather than later. Consistency is key.

6. Victimhood

In truth, many people play the victim card at one point or another. Your story of trauma, cultural or childhood conditioning, unfortunate circumstances or lack of resources doesn't serve you well if you stay in it.

Victimhood creates the excuses you use for not growing and moving forward. Many have had pretty crappy circumstances that could easily hold them back and sometimes do. Victimhood toys with your mindset, realigns your thoughts and relationships with a negative bent, and prevents you from making changes that will result in greater success.

Victims don't change the world. Overcomers do.

Release your attachment to victimhood and adopt the practices of those who overcome. Learn what you can from your circumstances and make the lessons part of the change you seek.

7. Control

The quicker you learn how little you have, the easier it will be to proceed.

As humans, we have an innate desire to control outcomes and circumstances. Loss of control is terribly frightening, and many fold under the pressure. Unproductive activities such as worry rarely serves you well. The quest for certainty can paralyze you when you're deciding how to move forward.

By believing that you will be supported, your desire to manipulate the outcome decreases significantly because you believe it will be supported regardless. Surrendering control is probably the most affirmative declaration of confidence you can engage in.

Spotlight: Cheryl LaTray

Cheryl LaTray is an amazing example of subtracting that which does not serve her well. She makes her desires reality by keeping the negativity that could prevent them at bay. Inspiring excellence is what she strives for everyday and succeeds.

"You are not defined by what happens to you. You are defined by the character you build within you. " ~ Cheryl LaTray

This quote adorns the wall of Cheryl LaTray's real estate office. Cheryl is an incredibly savvy real estate broker. Within the industry, she is respected for her resilience and work ethic. Her strength of character is a result of her circumstances.

Cheryl is a single mom of seven children who used real estate to support her family. She works tirelessly to inspire and be an example of perseverance, strength and fortitude for not only her family, but the community and all those around her. Cheryl's inspirational nature and willingness to give has been recognized again and again. One of her proudest moments was being chosen to carry the Olympic torch, nominated by those who witnessed her optimistic attitude and tireless work ethic on a daily basis.

Like many of the spotlights in this book, Cheryl was hesitant about being spotlighted for her confidence. Her company is currently expanding and, as with any expansion, there is discomfort. She reminds herself of the gold fish theory. The gold fish will expand to fit its surroundings. When it is transferred to a bigger tank it will eventually grow to fit the bowl, but there is a time of being a small fish in a big bowl and it may not feel safe or comfortable. When you want to grow, you have to become comfortable with being uncomfortable. This concept is one Cheryl lives by and one she wished to share.

Recently when she did an office expansion, Cheryl was feeling a little nostalgic. She had a few moments of what could be defined as momentary fear and insecurity around the risk of expanding. Recalling herself as a young girl who sat at her decked out desk with her new typewriter and created business plans, defining goals and dreams for fun, Cheryl marveled that she no longer had one only desk, but a whole office suite of them! She is making her dreams of youth a reality.

Cheryl not only uses recollections from the past to keep her focused, but also practices connecting with her "future" self. Her five-years-from-now self can remind her that she will make it through the discomfort of her present situation as well as give her an idea of what she may learn and accomplish as a result. Eliminating some of the fear of the unknowns allows for much greater risk taking.

Cheryl is all about give back, striving to live authentically, and to inspire others through her example. She regularly mentors others and shares the skills and strategies that have helped her achieve success today. Cheryl has a love of business plans and understands the importance of creating a life plan.

- What kind of life do you want to lead?
- What do you want to accomplish?
- What kind of legacy do you want to leave?
- What kind of character will define you?

As Cheryl has discovered, when you concentrate on fulfilling your life plan, business success falls into place.

Filling the Unoccupied Space

Once you've made space by subtracting that which does not serve you well, begin the process of filling the unoccupied space – slowly. Adding too much too soon causes overwhelm and then stagnation. You'll remain stuck in the mediocrity you are trying to eliminate because the changes are too overwhelming. Remember how to eat an elephant – one bite at a time.

1. Consistent Action

This probably goes without saying, but ideas and opportunities will not become a reality until you take action. Confidence stems from the action word TRUST! If you don't trust, developing confidence will not become your reality.

Remember the path from fear into confidence:

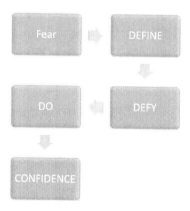

Each step requires an action that requires your attention. You can have thoughts all day long, but without acting, they will rarely become a reality.

Here is the thing about action though. Keep it as consistent as possible. Consistency creates reliability. Reliability creates trust. People will do business with those that consistently and reliably meet their needs. Putting systems in place to create consistency is crucial for growth.

2. Accountability partner

It takes discipline to be an entrepreneur. An accountability partner may be the answer to keeping you on track.

If you don't have a colleague to help you out, start journaling, create your own mastermind, hire a coach, or join a group. There are plenty of ways to create accountability.

Accountability partners tie into the feedback loop and help with goal setting and planning. They can be the fresh set of eyes that will see the things you miss. Entrepreneurship can be tough. Don't be afraid to seek the support, encouragement and positive feedback you need for growth.

3. Gratitude

This is a big one. If you want to attract abundance practice gratitude.

Gratitude amplifies abundance. When you're grateful for all of the outcomes, resources and needs that are met regardless of how small they may seem, you send a signal that what you have is enough. You will attract more with every act or whisper of gratitude.

4. Self-Care

Filling your needs is vitally important. If you're depleted, you have less to give. When you're fulfilled, you have more to give.

This is big challenge for entrepreneurs, especially those who are using a lot of masculine energy. Let me write one more email. Let me make one more phone call. I-can-sleep-when-I-die type of attitudes just cause burnout.

You need to set firm boundaries here. Taking care of yourself is a must.

Self-care may conjure up thoughts of spa days, but it can also involve:

- Eating healthy
- Getting enough rest
- Exercising/moving your body
- Practicing gratitude
- Keeping a journal
- Learning a new skill
- Engaging in a new hobby
- Meditating
- Reading daily devotionals
- Playing and having fun
- Laughing
- Relaxing
- Being creative
- Enjoying healthy relationships
- Getting organized

Most of the entrepreneurs engaged in exercise. It builds the stamina and energy needed to go the distance in entrepreneurship. The other self-care activity that most of them practiced was massage. This allowed them the opportunity to receive. Entrepreneurs by nature are givers and can be uncomfortable receiving. Massage is a good way to be reminded that it is okay to receive sometimes too.

Make self-care a priority. It will pay you back tenfold.

5. Knowledge

To grow, you need to learn and study. It doesn't always involve getting degrees or certifications. Sometimes finding a mentor is enough, not to mention the education you receive from your experiences. Knowledge is power, and however you acquire it will be a benefit.

I developed a new appreciation for this when I attended James Malinchak's Big Money Speaker Boot Camp. He shared that he studied the big speakers before him to capture their practices so he could recreate them for himself.

This is something I took to heart. I have chosen one of the most challenging job titles in the world. I had many mentors tell me not to adopt the title THE Confidence Coach. It would be hard to get clients because no one wants to admit they don't have confidence. They were right. It is a challenge.

This is not a woe-is-me tale. It is a demonstration of where study really paid off. I chose to study how professionals that came before me talked about polarizing and uncomfortable subjects. One of my favorites was Dr. Brene Brown. I studied how she talked about vulnerability and shame without talking about them.

I applied much of what I learned in my current marketing strategy and it has made a significant difference for me.

Observing the behaviors and practices of those that came before you is an option always available to you. You actually are already in engaged in that action. Isn't that exactly what you are doing by reading this book?

6. Course Correction

The entrepreneurial journey is rarely one of a straight and narrow path. There will be dips and valleys, and there will be times when you need to change direction to serve your best interest. Often the entrepreneurial path looks like this:

You might be straying from your original *why*. You may realize that your *why* has changed. You may not be able to make your enterprise financially viable and it's time to try something else. There are many reasons to course-correct and you may even feel that the only option is to get off the path all together. It is okay. It's normal. Just realize that every dip, valley, and uphill climb is designed to prepare you for a burst of brilliance.

Very few of the entrepreneurs in this book are doing the exact same thing as when they started out. They were confident enough to begin with an idea, but they were also confident enough to change that idea. Refinement, re-focusing, and innovation all contribute to course corrections. The entrepreneur that cannot see another way lacks confidence.

7. Investment

When you view any situation with the "investment" lens, it creates much greater clarity. Ask yourself: Will this investment of time, money, and energy yield an acceptable return?

If the return on investment is acceptable, proceed. If not, look at the conditions that need to change to yield a better return. Maybe the answer is complete course correction or maybe just a minor shift. The important thing is to be able to analyze quickly before investing your valuable resources.

Viki Winterton shared that she will always assess the profitability of a project before she proceeds. It is important to decide if a particular project will contribute to your goals and growth before saying yes! Balance of investment and return are vital for growth as an entrepreneur.

8. Personality

Let your personality and your experience show. Embrace the freedom of who you are and let that be its own selling point. This is what makes you different from the crowd. Give yourself permission to discover, develop and use your personality to connect with others.

Do not be afraid to be who you are. Your personality and experiences will be a point of connection for the audience you are meant to serve.

9. Empathy

Your life experiences will connect you to the people you're trying to reach. Your ability to identify with others will provide a clear path for connection. Brene Brown tells us that the most important words a person can hear, are "Me too."

None of us want to be isolated, invisible, or unheard. Showing empathy is an excellent way to breed connection. Use this for both others and yourself. The most profound shifts for me happened when I exercised empathy rather than harsh judgment on myself.

10. Resilience

Resilience is cultivated from trials and challenges. It's all about getting up more often than you get knocked down. Resilience shows a copious amount of confidence because you know you have what it takes to get back on your feet.

Confidence does not mean charmed. It does not assure you a life free from pain or strife. It does not equate to easy. It does provide you the security of knowing you will be supported throughout all of it. Confidence makes getting up so much easier.

Spotlight: Therese Skelly

Therese Skelly accepted many of the stories she had been conditioned to believe about herself. She began achieving real success when she started embracing her personality and experiences, which only served to increase her capacity for empathy and connection. She is a rock star example of how this works to your advantage as an entrepreneur.

Therese Skelly, the "Happy in Business Coach," is an accidental entrepreneur. She was a psychotherapist before she became the Happy In Business Coach she is now.

One day she was reading an ad in the newspaper asking for business coaches. Therese had no experience as a business coach, but the ad leapt off the page and she felt called to apply. She followed her intuition and landed the position.

Therese is a true creative, but also a phenomenal business coach. Her right brain, feminine tendencies could be detrimental to her business growth, but she put a project management system into place to assist her with follow–through, details, and execution of tasks for the programs she offers. Her desire to create and serve is so strong that having a team in place is vital for maintaining her Guidance (Yes, with a capital G) centered focus and not being bogged down in the details.

There were several times in Therese's career when she felt held back. Sometimes it was mindset, like not owning her value or having unhealed wounds and shame. Other times it was not having a structure in place for follow-up strategies and project management.

The combination of mindset and lack of structure led to her bankruptcy at one point. She could have packed her bags and found a job, but she didn't. Therese wholeheartedly believes in the words of Michael Beckwith, "Life happens for you, not against you."

Sharing her experiences has helped Therese serve her clients in a much bigger and better way. Her resiliency and faith in what she was called to learn, so she could then teach, has resulted in amazing connections that are paramount to her and a six-figure income.

Therese lives and practices boldly and has learned to stay true to her personality. She acts with as much authenticity as possible and is a great example of creating a positive flow of energy so she can move forward.

One ideal that Therese holds dear is her "freedom at all costs" motivation. Having the freedom to create her own schedule, create a flow of money, etc., matters more than the security a "job" might deliver. Some people are driven by the need for safety over freedom, but Therese is not one of them. In fact, most entrepreneurs are not.

Therese urges entrepreneurs to never give up! If the life of an entrepreneur is truly what you are called to do, burn the ship! The universe will be clear about your intention and step up to support you.

Therese shared a story of going to a conference of leaders with seven-figure businesses. One night they were dancing, and most were dancing with wild abandon. They were fully embracing the moment with all the energy they could muster. Therese made the connection of needing to be all in – in your life and your business. These seven-figure earners approach their businesses with the same wild abandon as their dancing and are creating outstanding results.

When you choose to be all in and release the obstacles in your way, the results speak for themselves.

Tools for the Tool Chest

The entrepreneurial journey can be tough at times. You are building something that didn't exist before. That takes a certain amount of skill. Confidence is the main tool that helps you build the rest. Here are some other tools to keep tucked in as you move forward.

1. The Zebra Moment

A zebra moment? What's that?

A Zebra Moment is *why* you do what you do.

It is the epiphany when you realize that the message you feel called to give is more important than the discomfort of sharing it.

Entrepreneurship can be uncomfortable. You will face rejection, frustration, confusion, and disorder in your business. If your *why* is not strong enough, making it through those tough spells becomes harder and the business may fold under the pressure. When the *why* is strong - when you can hardly stand to keep the offering, message, product or service to yourself - then you'll have a constant source of inspiration that will see you through the rough patches.

All of the successful, confident entrepreneurs in this book had a compelling zebra moment - an event or moment that makes their discomfort in their entrepreneurial pursuits worth it. I chose these entrepreneurs mostly because of their *why*. They all touched me in some way.

Most entrepreneurs have more than one zebra moment. New moments occur as their *why* evolves. My most profound zebra moment was in that space between a rock and a hard place and the choice I made that day. I felt hopeless and desperate, but when I realized I had choices, everything changed for me.

I determined that day that no one else would ever feel that hopelessness in his or her life if I had anything to do with it. Whenever I get frustrated that things aren't growing fast enough or I feel rejected because something I was hoping for falls through, I remember back to that day and the commitment I made to myself to share the valuable lesson I learned. Hopelessness is quite possibly the worst feeling in the world. I would not want anyone to experience if I can help it.

I asked a few fellow entrepreneurs to share their zebra moments. I think it's important to understand your *why*, and these ladies were kind enough to share theirs. Their stories, written in their voice, may give you some inspiration to define your own Zebra Moment. If you haven't done it yet, it is vital to move forward.

Kim Boudreau Smith

I have had so many "ah-ha" moments in my life. Some have been small that led to life changing ones, and those, in turn, led me to where I am now.

Many years ago, I was in corporate America. I was climbing up that corporate ladder, so to speak; however, I always had this feeling like I was a caged animal - unable to get off that ladder with no freedom.

My positions were always in sales and marketing management, where it was numbers, numbers, numbers. Time didn't matter. Only numbers! It was great because this felt somewhat like my own business. I could come and go as I pleased and set my own hours. Everything was predicated on the numbers. It really was fantastic, but something was missing. It was passion, the love of doing something I cared about. My first business was birthed in a gym at a fitness company. I was good at it and I had a passion for it. I realized I was finally in heaven, owning my own business. My confidence grew, but I kept hitting a wall.

The "life changing wall" came to me seven years ago when I fell asleep at a major intersection, not once but twice. The red light at that intersection changed my life. I had been a successful business owner with a wonderful fitness business, but I was looking for more. I was looking outside of me, where my confidence begins, and I found I was just running in circles.

It was then that I had an epiphany. I decided to acquire a life-coaching certification and complete other things in my life that were left undone. I wanted to help others with the same struggles I was having. I used that coaching certification to launch another business: Coaching for Women Entrepreneurs. But my phone didn't ring. I was struggling and it was definitely playing on my confidence. Again, I was on the outside and not listening to my true heart's desire, MY voice. I was not in alignment with myself and could see I was doing a bit of forcing.

Time passed and I knew I was missing something in my business. I needed to get my message out there. I really enjoy talking more than writing (another small epiphany...) so off I went and launched a radio show. Of course I had no idea this would lead to eventually owning Bold Radio Station. There are no coincidences here; my belief is the voice/sound is so healing and power-filled. Giving others the ability to experience what I have experienced, using your voice, is awesome. It is so empowering, inspiring, and uplifting to be a part of others doing the same. There is so much magic in a voice. We can heal, uplift and transform others and spread love through our voice. This is much better than the hurt, destruction and spreading of hate through our words that we tend to hear too much. This was the biggest "ah-ha" moment in my life, and putting myself out there at this level is definitely a daily confidence builder.

There is no Plan B and no turning back. And I wouldn't have it any other way!

Abby Kohut

I'll never forget the day I became "Absolutely Abby," not by name but in my heart. I had been a recruiter for about 12 years. I had hired thousands of people and I had become used to the familiarity of rejecting the people I couldn't hire. I would send them rejection letters essentially saying, "We found a better candidate for the job." The letter didn't tell them why. I couldn't tell them why.

One day I decided to tell a candidate why. She had answered a question in a way that made the hiring manager nervous that she would leave in a year. I realized that telling people why would help them land a new job faster. By telling them the absolute truth, I could change someone's life because they would get back to being a productive member of society, which job seekers yearn for.

I was there in 2008. I yearned for it too. In 2008, I hosted a job search event in Manhattan. I wrote my first book the weekend before the event and copied it at Staples. Fifteen people bought my book and asked me to autograph it. What a huge honor!

Later that year I attended a seminar taught by best-selling author Dr. Barbara De Angelis. She said over and over, "The world is waiting for your words." I cried like a baby because I knew she was right. When I returned home from the event, I considered different domains for my new business. Among the candidates were AbbyUnplugged.com, AbbyAbbreviated.com, and ActuallyAbby.com. Thanks to my friends and family members, AbsolutelyAbby.com was born in 2009.

When I started to write articles on my new site, the words just spilled out from my heart. I had waited so long to tell the absolute truth and now I could do it on my terms and with my personality. But wait...could I? What if the world didn't like my opinions or my ideas? What if people had comments? I continued to write and found that although people had different opinions, it was actually OK. I wrote 126 blog posts which eventually helped me write my second book, Absolutely Abby's 101 Job Search Secrets.

Writing was great but I knew that I had to do more. I had to speak to job seekers and teach them what other recruiters didn't tell them. I taught them my secrets and they were grateful.

I will never forget the day that a job seeker in NJ told me that I was the best speaker she had ever heard. Dumbfounded, I asked her what she was talking about. She said that I was just "real." I was down to earth and I didn't talk down to anyone like other job search speakers do. That was the single best gift I have received as a speaker. That is the day I embraced my "realness."

In 2012, I bought an RV and began the Absolutely Abby Job Search Success Tour. Now I educate job seekers in cities all around the U.S. Am I still afraid of saying or writing the wrong thing? Absolutely! I believe every entrepreneur is. But without taking the risk of stepping on the stage, I can't make as much of an impact. So, I step on it day after day. I am forever Absolutely Abby and I am Absolutely grateful!

Christine Baker Marriage

I was tired.

No, I wasn't just tired. I was exhausted. I was overwhelmed.

Initially I had been excited to fly out to LA from my home in Western New York to attend this conference, but now I was questioning why I was there.

You see, I'm a Licensed Massage Therapist. (A damn good one, I might add.) And here I was at a boot camp for paid speakers.

And I wasn't a speaker. In fact for the past several years, I would have done almost anything to avoid the spotlight. Coordinating the logistics for this trip had been a nightmare. Arranging child care, coordinating their transportation, rescheduling my clients, buying new luggage, etc. had all taken their toll.

I was reminded of my years struggling as a single parent. Up until this trip I had not really shared my personal story. I was uncomfortable owning it to be honest. No one knows quite what to say when they hear that my husband at age 37 died suddenly leaving me (age 30) with four kids under 8. It was hard for me to share the struggles, the sleepless nights, and the incredible deep heartache that truly can't be explained, especially without being emotional even 13 years later. I was certain that no one wanted or needed to hear about the profound loss that I had experienced. That is why I had never really "revealed" where I was coming from. What made my loss special enough to share it?

Choices to Changes

After years struggling to find my purpose beyond raising my children, I stumbled upon massage therapy. Within a week, I had attended an information session, applied for a student loan and enrolled in massage school. 18 months later, I was a licensed massage therapist and dedicated my life to improving the health and wellness of others.

And the first few years had been great.

But a funny thing happens when you give of yourself constantly for years. You begin to burn out.

I still had the need to give back, but providing wellness services one one-hour-session at a time was leaving me exhausted and unfulfilled.

And as much as I hoped this trip would recharge my batteries, instead I felt overwhelmed.

It was in that hotel room that Sheila, my dear friend, verbally slapped me right upside my head.

"You have experienced profound loss. But, look at all that you have accomplished! Look at all that you have become from that loss. Look at the success you have experienced. Look at all that your experience has taught you!"

It was at that moment that I realized that these life experiences didn't have to define who I wasn't, but could contribute to who I could become. All the struggles of business were made easier from what I learned through personal trials. I had never made that connection before.

Sheila reminded me to take in the seminar and everything it had to offer. There were some truly impressive speakers and my fellow students were equally inspiring.

126

It was time.

Time to be clear about what I was now called to do.

Bodywork would no longer my focus. As much as I loved working with people to reach their wellness goals, I understood now that I was called to reach a greater audience.

It was time to share how my personal and professional experiences integrated with each other to propel me into becoming a successful and seasoned business owner.

It was time to teach others how to create their own success. It was time to shed my insecurities and step out onto the stage.

2. Visualization

Visualization is particularly useful when weighing your options and trying to make a decision. Picture the worst-case scenario and the best-case scenario, and you'll have created a spectrum by which you can make a decision.

3. Affirmations

Bert Martinez transformed the worst producing sales team to the top producers in nine months. How? By using affirmations.

There is a variety of ways for you to engage in affirmations. Verbalizing your affirmations, using mirror love, creating vision boards, listening to audios, podcasts or music, using mementos like jewelry, tattoos, accessories or other talisman to take you to time when you felt complete and quite possibly unstoppable. Reliving those sentiments regularly can help you affirm similar or even better outcomes.

I am firmly opposed to a "fake it 'til you make it" mentality. I do, believe, however, in creating intention. The problem is that the words you say may not be in alignment with your subconscious beliefs. Many times using affirmations can feel inauthentic and the result won't materialize.

I would rather see someone dive into personal development and emerge confidently, but I will concede that affirmations can create the space for you to step into an intention and shine.

4. Celebrations

I am not advocating popping the champagne cork every time you have a successful outcome. There is much more to celebrating than that.

The reason celebration is so important is that positive reinforcement creates a pleasure pathway in your brain that connects an action to a desired response. For example, if making decisions is tough for you, then celebrate making the decision, not the outcome of the decision.

Celebrating close to the action you want to reward is incredibly beneficial. Waiting a week to celebrate will still create a pleasure pathway in the brain, but your brain most likely will not associate what you're celebrating if you let too much time elapse. Even a momentary acknowledgment, like an imaginary fist bump or high five, may be all you need to celebrate until something more profound takes place.

The other benefit to celebrating is that when you decide how to celebrate, you're identifying your internal motivators. This is extremely valuable when you take risks. It's all part of knowing yourself and what triggers you to perform and achieve greater success.

Try making a list of the ways you would celebrate. They can be low cost and even no cost. Write them on pieces of paper and put them in a celebration jar to pull out every time you celebrate. Using a visual such as this will keep it top of mind practice.

5. Positive self-talk

Choose your words carefully when you describe yourself and your business. Words and thoughts set the intention, so why not make it positive?

The negative voices that may emerge are your body's mechanism to keep you safe and remain in your comfort zone. When you hear negativity creeping in, try thanking it for showing up, acknowledging its efforts at keeping you safe, and then quietly explain that you're OK. Dismiss them before they get the upper hand.

6. Journals and recordings

Keeping a record of how you think, feel, and behave helps you recognize and evaluate progress. I wrote *You Had It All Along* as a journal filled with activities because I wanted to have a record to refer back to.

Journaling can lead to self-discovery. Growth is impossible without evaluation, and journaling is a great way to measure it. If you are not comfortable writing, make a video or an audio to play at a later time.

7. Retreats and meditation

This does not have to be the way you typically think of retreat. Karen McMillan, the Retreat Muse, teaches about the value of a short mind retreat. Slowing down to get centered and focused and even just breathing for a few minutes can have major impact on your productivity and creativity.

You may want to meditate or retreat in a variety of ways. It might be something really fun like taking a bowlful of sand from your last beach vacation and keeping it in your office space. When you feel the need to retreat you can run your hands through the sand to reconnect to the happiness you found on the beach. Retreat can also be as elaborate as going on a spa vacation for a few days. You get to choose what is appropriate and what fills your needs.

8. Play

So many entrepreneurs use their masculine energy to be productive and struggle with playing. Play seems frivolous and pointless. I will argue that play allows you to be more creative and innovative, therefore giving it a purpose.

If you need a reason to play, connect it to enhanced creativity and innovation. I encourage you to explore what play means to you.

9. Inquisitiveness

Be curious. Ask *why?*

Curiosity helps define clarity. It helps in recognizing value. It helps in defining needs. It helps in more ways than you can imagine.

Get comfortable asking meaningful questions that elicit thoughtful responses. If your job as an entrepreneur is to facilitate the change process, you'll need to ask good questions to monitor your progress and the progress of those you serve.

10. Appreciate the Ordinary

Are you missing everyday miracles in your life because you're so focused on extraordinary ones (or the lack thereof)? If so, it's time to stop.

How often do you find yourself searching for or building the next best thing to make you money? There is simplicity in ordinary things that you do every day that could yield you huge returns if you repurpose them and offer them attractively.

When I first heard Jeff Hoffman speak, he talked about his "think like a five-year-old days". He directed his employees to spend a day going back to basics and asking the question *why?* The results were profound. Processes were streamlined, money was saved, creativity was reborn, and the entire climate of the company changed just by noticing the ordinary things that no one had paid attention to.

Choices to Changes

Try repurposing simple things and offer them for a fee. Change it up by bundling your packages. It doesn't always have to about bells and whistles. Sometimes the simpler, the better.

Spotlight: Bert Martinez

Bert Martinez gets it. When you use the tools available to you, coupled with the intersection of mindset, connections and structure, you get great results. Bert is a magnet for not only his own success, but for the results he helps his clients create.

Bert Martinez is a money-making problem-solver. He spends his time generating income for entrepreneurs and companies that want to make more money. He has achieved success both financially and personally. His wisdom and practices are born from the ebb and flow of his entrepreneurship and are part of the charm and value he brings to the table.

Bert begins every day at the gym and then reads scripture, plays a game, and eats breakfast with his wife and children before they head off to school. He begins each day giving attention to the most important things in his life – his family, his health, and his spirituality. No matter what happens the rest of the day, the most valued aspects of his life have been addressed.

Bert recognizes how important the *why* is for people. Even though his *why* evolves over time, he reviews it daily along with his goals. He says, **"A *why* that is weak will produce results that are weak."**

Bert has seen plenty of evidence to prove the importance of a strong *why* as an entrepreneur, and he teaches that lesson to his clients.

Knowing your *why* makes all of the difference because when the *why* is most important, obstacles become irrelevant. Bert shared the example of an abuse victim who finally decides to leave her abuser. Her obstacles of not knowing where to go, how she will support herself, etc., become secondary to the main objective: just getting out. When the *why* is strong, you will find a way.

One of the ways Bert facilitates growth is by using affirmations. Every statement you make becomes an affirmation of the intention behind it. Even negative statements become an affirmation or confirmation of truth. Bert purchases door hangers and writes his affirmations on them. He hangs them from the rearview mirror, on door handles, and has even laminates them to put in the shower. As he cleans his body, he cleans his mind.

The affirmations certainly work. Bert transformed the worst producing sales team to a record-producing sales team in less than a year by having them recite affirmations with emotional intensity twice a day. When the company that hired him adopted the use of affirmations as company policy, revenue doubled in less than two years. What an excellent affirmation of the power of this practice.

Bert urges entrepreneurs to make mistakes faster. The quicker you make mistakes, the quicker you get to the opportunity that presents as a result. He's learned his most profound lessons from his mistakes.

Before he was thirty, Bert made millions, only to lose it all by the time he was 31. During the rebuilding process, he saw the opportunities to learn from his mistakes and applied those lessons. Clearly his ability to see the opportunities born from mistakes has changed the course of his career and his life.

Humility has replaced arrogance. Service to others has replaced acquiring trophies. Now Bert uses the fear he may experience as a motivator to jump-start his courage to play an even bigger game and be more of a blessing to others.

Choices to Changes

A Few Final Observations

Confident entrepreneurs practice differently, but they do share some common traits:

- They're comfortable taking risks and are not paralyzed by indecision.

- They step quickly out of the spin of insecurity.

- They choose to put it all on the line to promote the idea or product that changes themselves, the marketplace, and their personal and global economies. If they are passionate and excellent communicators, they also change the way people think, feel, and behave.

- They're leaders willing to go against the grain because they follow an instinct that says business as usual is not the only way to influence the world.

- They choose to separate from the crowd because being alone means they can stand out, and sometimes becoming the solo voice in a noisy marketplace is exactly what's necessary to create real change.

They almost seem too good to be true don't they?

Maybe, but they are human. Every one of the entrepreneurs in this book has had moments when they've slipped in their practice of confident entrepreneurship. Each one has had to overcome obstacles. They have fallen down and gotten back up. They keep going and don't give up. Why? Because at the end of the day, they trust in an outcome they cannot see and that they will be supported regardless of what the outcome is.

Everything has a way of working out when you believe it can.

They trust that they don't always have to know how the resources will look, but they can choose to open the space for them to arrive.

Remember as you go forth that these are *practices*. Practice creates mastery. Some will be a fit for you and others will not. Adopt the ones that work for you and enjoy the changes they will make. Then move on to the next set. Remember to reserve negative judgment and make changes at a relatively comfortable pace. Stretching too fast and too far out of your comfort zone will not yield the best results.

Overhauling everything at once usually creates overwhelm and frustration. Take your time. Start where you can and make the best of what you already possess. Avoid the negative rabbit hole of judgment when it doesn't come together as quickly as you would like. I know you are in a hurry to grow, but rushing ahead usually results in having to go back and start again.

Remember that growth hurts. It requires you to shed your skin. You will make mistakes along the way. You will fall. The harder you fall, the higher you will rise. Welcome it. It means better things are coming.

Writing this book was an unexpected demonstration of that for me. After my 60-day experiment in using these practices, I thought I had cracked the code for success. Things were going smoothly and I felt like success was finally mine. I loved my new clients. I was making more money than ever before. I was writing a book, and I accepted speaking engagements for the first time in more than a year. Things were as settled in my personal life as they had been in years. I felt like I had it all.

Then I was reminded in short order what happens when you up-level. To acquire the tools and strength to enjoy a new level, you will be tested. Those new challenges prepare you for what comes next. In my case, that meant everything started falling apart.

I will spare you the details, but as a result, I learned the lessons I share in this book in a deeply personal way. I have learned:

- Confidence is a journey, not a destination.

- The presence of fear and doubt do not mean a lack of confidence. It means you get to be strategic about how long you let them set up camp and stay.

- You won't take risks if you don't trust your judgment due to poor decisions made in the past. Remember that you made the best decisions you could with what you knew at the time. Judging those decisions based on newly acquired knowledge is counterproductive.

- Feedback from accountability partners and mentors is essential. It is vital to have someone hold the mirror for you to see what is happening in your life and business. A fresh set of eyes can be a really good thing.

- Make peace with the stories that shape you. The peace will create a light that makes you wildly attractive to those you are meant to serve. Those stories can only tarnish you if you let them. Let your brilliance shine.

- View each moment as a gift. Choose to unwrap it. Learn from it. Grow because of it. Share it.

- Success most often comes down to your why and your clarity around it. When you're passionate about your why, sharing it becomes as necessary as breathing. Find that passion. Remind yourself of it every day and before each encounter.

I also learned that although confident entrepreneurship provides many freedoms, you are never free from the darkness that occasionally shows up. Be confident that it has a purpose. It is through darkness that you'll discover an even brighter light if you choose to welcome what it has to teach you.

While writing this book I learned, for the second time in my life, that sometimes your world falls apart. I could have chosen to stay buried under the rubble or use it as a fortress to protect myself. Instead, I chose to use the rubble to build a staircase to higher ground. The view is much better from here.

You have the power to choose.

Embrace your entrepreneurial choices today. They shape the changes the world will make tomorrow. That is wickedly powerful!

Entrepreneurship is tough, but you can be tougher.

Let your legacy be defined by what you did, not by what you were too afraid to try. Find courage to make choices and trust that you will be supported through the resulting changes.

Accept the responsibility and risk that confident entrepreneurship begs of you and enjoy the fruits of your efforts. Discover your sweet spot, subtract what doesn't serve you, add what does, use the tools and resources you already have available to you and revel in the freedom that entrepreneurship provides.

You have everything you need, including support you may not always recognize. In fact, **you had it all along**.

Spotlight Resources

Viki Winterton	www.expertinsightspublishing.com
Jeff Hoffman	www.colorjar.com
David Dey	www.institute4se.com
Karen McMillan	www.kdmcmillan.com
Forbes Riley	www.forbesriley.com
	www.forbesfactor.com
Sarah Newton	www.theyouthexpert.com
Keefe Duterte	www.keefespeaks.com
Joie Gharrity	www.113branding.com
Brooks Hoffos	www.FuseRealty.ca
Cheryl LaTray	www.jazzyspeaker.com
Therese Skelly	www.happyinbusiness.com
Bert Martinez	www.bertmartinez.com

Kim Boudreau Smith	www.kimbsmith.com
Abby Kohut	www.absolutelyabby.com
Christine Baker Marriage	www.ccbakermarriage.com

Choices to Changes

Book List

The following book list includes titles from those spotlighted or referred to in this book. A (+) after an author's name indicates that the book is a compilation and has more than one contributor.

Scale: Seven Proven Principles to Grow Your Business and Get Your Life Back ... by Jeff Hoffman and David Finkel

Beyond Your Book ... Viki Winterton

Ready, Aim, Inspire ... Viki Winterton +

Ready, Aim, Captivate ... Viki Winterton +

Ready, Aim, Influence ... Viki Winterton, Keefe Duterte +

Ready, Aim, Soar ... Viki Winterton +

Ready, Aim, Impact ... Viki Winterton +

Ready, Aim, Excel ... Viki Winterton +

The Teen Years - Don't Get Mad - Get Through It: A Parent's Guide ... Sarah Newton

Help! My Teenager is an Alien: The Everyday Situation Guide for Parents ... Sarah Newton

Impactology: Unleash Your Genius and Change the World ... Sarah Newton

Millionaire Mom's in the Making ... Therese Skelly +

Trust Your Heart: Building Relationships that Build Your Business ... *Therese Skelly* +

Corporate Mom Drop Outs ... Therese Skelly +

It's Not How You Start It's How You Finish ... Keefe Duterte

Choices to Changes

Hire and Grow Rich (January Release) ... Bert Martinez

How To Pitch Reporters ... Bert Martinez

Bold is Beautiful: Kindness Beauty & Strength ... Kim Boudreau Smith +

Bold is Beautiful: Breakthrough to Business Strategies ... Kim Boudreau Smith, Therese Skelly +

Success in High Heels ... Kim Boudreau Smith +

Hot Mama in High Heels ... Kim Boudreau Smith +

Manifesting in High Heels ... Kim Boudreau Smith +

The Missing Piece: A Transformational Journey ... Kim Boudreau Smith +

The Missing Piece: In Business ... Kim Boudreau Smith +

Absolutely Abby's 101 Job Search Secrets ... Abby Kohut

Absolutely Abby's Top 12 Interview Questions Exposed ... Abby Kohut

Fabulous at Fifty ... Abby Kohut +

The Gifts of Imperfection ... Dr. Brene Brown

Daring Greatly ... Dr. Brene Brown

UnMarketing ... Scott Stratten

Multipliers ... Liz Wiseman

B ... Sarah Kay

You Had It All Along ... Sheila Kennedy

About the Author

Sheila Kennedy is THE Confidence Coach. From insecure, divorced, and struggling single mom to best-selling author, speaker and coach, Sheila influences entrepreneurs around the globe. She shares skills, tools and strategies that turns confidence into gaining visibility, building meaningful relationships, taking bigger risks and growing financially for entrepreneurs and their business.

An entrepreneur for 8+ years, Sheila has learned that one's level of confidence directly impacts success in the marketplace. Her new book, **Choices to Changes**, details practices, tools and strategies for successful entrepreneurship. The book features Twelve Global Entrepreneurs that enjoy the profitability, freedom and fulfillment that entrepreneurship promises and confidence delivers.

Find out more about the work she does by visiting www.confidenceatyourcore.com.

49923137R00081

Made in the USA
Charleston, SC
09 December 2015